COVENANT: THE HISTORY
OF A BIBLICAL IDEA

DELBERT R. HILLERS

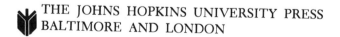 THE JOHNS HOPKINS UNIVERSITY PRESS
BALTIMORE AND LONDON

The Johns Hopkins University Press, Baltimore, Maryland 21218
The Johns Hopkins Press Ltd., London

Originally published, 1969

Johns Hopkins paperback edition, 1969
Second printing, 1970
Third printing, 1973
Fourth printing, 1974
Fifth printing, 1977

Library of Congress Catalog Card Number 69–13539
ISBN 0-8018-1010-8 (hardcover)
ISBN 0-8018-1011-6 (paperback)

Dedicated to
Professor William F. Albright

CONTENTS

PUBLISHER'S NOTE

The history of ideas as a form of scholarly inquiry took shape at The Johns Hopkins University in the first half of the century. The man chiefly responsible was Arthur O. Lovejoy, whose twenty-eight years as professor of philosophy were spent promoting the historiography of the intellect. With two colleagues, George Boas and Gilbert Chinard, he founded the History of Ideas Club, where, in an atmosphere at once congenial and critical, visiting scholars might offer their interpretations of the development of the great ideas that have influenced civilization. Lovejoy was instrumental in founding the *Journal of the History of Ideas* in pursuit of the same end. And in his own writings he persistently and patiently charted the transformations which a seminal idea might undergo—over time, across disciplines, or within the intellectual development of an individual thinker.

When, with Carnegie Corporation support, The Johns Hopkins University inaugurated an imaginatively new program of adult education in 1962, it was a happy inspiration to build it around a set of graduate seminars in the history of ideas; for the History of Ideas Club itself had long before been described as "a sort of seminar where mature men and women learned new and valuable lessons." To be sure, this evening program has followed Lovejoy's spirit of inquiry rather than his own actual practice. Not all the seminars are concerned to pursue in detail the transformations of a single unit-idea. Rather, there is a shared view that no theory—at any time, in any field—is simply self-generated, but that it springs by extension or opposition from earlier theories advanced in the field, or is borrowed from theories in cognate fields, or is derived from the blending of hitherto separate fields into one. To pursue the unfolding of any theory in these terms (so the teachers in the seminars believe) allows a sophisticated and rigorous discussion of contemporary scholarship with an audience lacking previous specified knowledge. These notions are an extension, not an abuse, of Lovejoy's concern; he had never wasted effort on being unduly prescriptive except to call, hopefully, for cooperative scholarship in a venture so clearly beyond the reasonable capabilities of a single scholar.

This series of books, *Seminars in the History of Ideas,* is intended to provide a wider audience with a chance to participate in "a sort of seminar" similar to those in the University's program. Just as the teaching seminars themselves draw on the spirit rather than merely the letter of Lovejoy's original enterprise, so this published series extends beyond those topics already offered in the University's program. But all, nonetheless, reflect that intent with which Lovejoy so long persisted in his own work: "the endeavor to investigate the history, and thereby, it may be hoped, to understand better the nature, of the workings of the human mind."

PREFACE

Mark Twain describes Aunt Polly's prayer as "built from the ground up of solid courses of Scriptural quotations, welded together with a thin mortar of originality." The present book is constructed in the same way, except that the mortar of originality is perhaps even thinner. Being an attempt to summarize for the common reader a very recent, and ongoing, discussion within Old Testament studies, it is dependent to an unusual degree on the researches of scholars still living and active. At this point I will mention only Professor George Mendenhall of the University of Michigan, whose writings have set off and directed much recent research into covenant ideas. But though I have drawn most heavily on Professor Mendenhall's works, I am also indebted to many other scholars to a degree that is difficult to acknowledge adequately, and I hope that the notes and suggestions for further reading will attract readers to consult their works, and give "honor to whom honor is due." I am conscious of coming especially short in giving credit to scholars whose contributions to our understanding of covenant ideas are not written in English; although I have used their works, for practical reasons I have referred readers only to books and articles in English.

Translations of Hebrew texts are my own. I have in general followed the practice of quoting biblical passages in full instead of simply supplying chapter and verse references, in the hope that readers will find this convenient.

Mr. James Rimbach, my student, read portions of the manuscript and made many suggestions and corrections and also prepared a draft on which the Suggestions for Further Reading is based. My colleague and teacher Professor Samuel

Iwry read the first chapter and in other ways helped me by giving generously of his time and advice. Mrs. Phyllis Rimbach not only typed the manuscript but, as secretary of the Department of Near Eastern Studies of The Johns Hopkins University, helped to free my time for work at it. I wish to express my thanks to them, and also to the staff of The Johns Hopkins Press, especially Mrs. Martha Bluming.

CHAPTER ONE

THE UNHAPPINESS OF OUR KNOWLEDGE

There are, as in Philosophy, so in Divinity, sturdy
doubts and boistrous objections, wherewith the
unhappiness of our knowledge too neerely acquainteth us.

Sir *Thomas Brown*, Religio Medici

A new study of the covenant between God and Israel requires some justification, for even a sympathetic reader may wonder whether such a familiar biblical theme really needs more explaining. A page in a Rabbinic Bible takes the form of a tiny raft of text afloat in a great sea of commentary, and even this only hints at the truly staggering amount of glossing to which the Scriptures have been subjected over the last two thousand years. It seems almost presumptuous to claim to have something new to say, especially when the topic is not Gog and Magog or the number of the Beast or some such perennial puzzle but an idea so central that it has provided the name for the two parts of the Christian Bible. I would seem to be one of those "commentators plain," of whom Crabbe complains, "Who from the dark and doubtful love to run, and hold their glimmering tapers to the sun."

Yet it is easy to see that "covenant" is just the sort of idea which is apt to become "dark and doubtful" with the passage of time. This will become clear if we consider some other examples of biblical language. (1) "I [God] will fall on them like a she-bear bereft of her cubs, and I will rip open their vitals" (Hosea 13:8). (2) "I [God] remember your devotion when you were young, your love as a bride, how you followed me in the wilderness, in the land that is not sown" (Jeremiah 2:2). (3) "Israel was a holy thing

belonging to Yahweh, the first of his produce. Any who
ate of him incurred guilt; calamity came upon them"
(Jeremiah 2:3).

Each of these passages contains an analogy. The relation of God to Israel is said to be like this or that within
human experience. But the kind of human experience which
is drawn on is different in each case, and therefore each
places a different demand on the reader or interpreter. The
first simile is so clear that it scarcely needs restatement: the
prophet says that God is going to destroy Israel in the spirit
and manner of a she-bear robbed of her young. But it is
worth asking why we cannot miss the point here. It is, of
course, because human experience of mother bears is much
the same in every age and every place. Scholarship adds
nothing. Hosea probably meant *ursus arctos syriacus*, but an
Eskimo understands him as well as an Israelite. Note also
that the analogy is explicit. The prophet makes it quite
clear that he is making a comparison; we do not merely
feel that he is doing so, for he himself would have called
this figurative language. Finally, this simile does not admit
of much extension. The prophets evidently had no scruples
about using theriomorphic language in speaking of God, any
more than they shared the embarrassment of some moderns
at anthropomorphisms. Hosea even gives us God as a moth.
But comparison of God to an angry bear was of limited
utility in expressing his relation to his people, and we do not
find passages expanding on the figure.

The second analogy differs from the first particularly in
this last respect. The idea that God and Israel are joined
as man and wife is obviously capable of extension in all kinds
of directions, and the Israelite writers exploit many of the
possibilities. Here in Jeremiah 2 we have the chaste and
ardent love of the honeymoon; elsewhere we find allusions
to the ornaments of the bride, the pet names from court-

ship days, and of course the subsequent unfaithfulness, Israel's paramours, and so on. "Where are your mother's divorce-papers?" the prophet writes, and the reader is expected to be familiar with the fundamental image of marriage between God and Israel. God as a she-bear is useful only once, for there is just one narrow point of resemblance, but God as Israel's husband is useful often and in many ways. Even so, we are right in regarding this also as a conscious use of figurative language. The Israelites did not really think that God was married to Israel. That is to say, they did not have a tradition that this had happened at some point in their past, or have a yearly celebration of the event as part of their liturgy. This second metaphor is also like the first in that it is drawn from an area of experience with which we are familiar. Not that Israelite marriage was just like modern American marriage, for many of the practices and attitudes differed from our own. But the fundamental resemblance is such that we will not miss the main point of most passages where this figure occurs.

The third metaphor is the most difficult for us. It is not drawn from ordinary human experience but from one particular portion of Israel's legal tradition, the law concerning first fruits. Each year at Pentecost (the Feast of Weeks) the first fruits of the harvest were brought to the sanctuary, as something holy, separated for divine use. If any man instead used the first fruits like the rest of the crop, he was guilty of sacrilege. And so, Jeremiah says, during the wilderness wanderings all Israel used to be like first fruits belonging to God, and anyone who "ate," this is, attacked, Israel committed sacrilege. Our understanding of the image depends on our information about this specific point of law.

"Yahweh[1] our God made a covenant with us in Horeb"

1. The Hebrew common noun for "god" is *Elohim*; it is used for the God of Israel and for other Gods. Israel's God also had a proper

(Deuteronomy 5:2). Taking this, or any passage referring to the covenant, we at once see that we are dealing with an analogy like those above. In the first place, a proportion is involved: just as a man may be joined with another man by a sworn agreement, so God is joined to Israel. But even without investigation we can say that the covenant metaphor has potentially much more in common with numbers two and three above than with number one. It is like the marriage analogy in that it is capable of being extended in many ways. A human alliance can be proposed, concluded, witnessed, committed to writing, broken, renewed, and so on and on, and any one of these features might be drawn on to express a religious idea. This means, too, that the basic image may often be present where the word is not. Just exactly which aspects of ancient covenant-making have been drawn into Israel's religious thought remains to be seen, of course, for at this point we can only weigh the possibilities,

---

name, the consonants of which were YHWH. Since the commandment forbade taking the name of God in vain, the custom arose in postexilic Judaism of not speaking the proper name of God at all, and though this did not happen overnight, eventually it became absolutely uniform practice. When a reader came across the consonants YHWH (Hebrew writing of the time generally indicated the consonants only, not the vowels), he said a different word, ʾadonay, meaning "Lord." When, in a much later time, well along into the Christian era, systems were developed for indicating in full the vowels of Hebrew words, either the vowels of YHWH had been forgotten or there was no desire to discover or record them. Instead, quite logically, the vocalizers put in the symbols that indicated the vowels for the word "Lord," ʾadonay, that being what was pronounced. The modern scholarly restoration of the ineffable name as "Yahweh" is based on ancient Greek transliterations and on the short forms of the name which are part of many personal names in the Bible: Yah, and Yahu. The ancient Greek and Latin versions translated the substitute-word, ʾadonay, and this became the common practice in English Bible versions, where LORD, in small capitals, means that YHWH stands in the Hebrew text. "Jehovah" is a late hybrid formed by taking the consonants of YHWH together with the vowels of ʾadonay.

but we may say in advance that we are apt to miss much if we look only at those texts where the term "covenant" itself occurs. The third metaphor cited above was drawn from the sphere of law, and it is plain that legal practice of some sort is the source of the covenant notion also. If we can discover the principles and practices connected with concluding legally binding pacts in ancient Israel and her neighbors, we will probably have the foundation for grasping the sense of the pact with God. This should perhaps also warn us not to expect a religious idea that is especially poetical or mystical, since the law tends to be short on poetry but long on precision.

Yet Israel's idea of a covenant with God differs from all of the above in important ways. It is much more than a figure of speech, at least in some periods. For all its frequency in the Scriptures, the picture of Israel as God's bride remained just that for the ancient Israelite: a picture, a sign pointing to something else. "Yahweh our God made a covenant with us in Horeb," however, referred to something that had actually happened—the text of the agreement was in a box in the temple. We may, for the sake of convenience, call this the history of a biblical idea, but quite obviously it was much more than an idea to Israel.

The covenant idea has been especially troublesome to interpreters of the Bible because of the lack of information about ancient covenants between men and between states. As stated before, we are dealing with a proportion: God is joined to Israel by a pact, just as one man may be joined to another. But there have been too many unknowns in this proportion to permit its solution. Just what was an ancient Israelite pact like? In the case of the analogy to the law about first fruits, the Bible itself provides sufficient clear evidence about the profane side of the equation; but as far as covenant is concerned, it does not. Scholars have, of course, tried to make do with information about modern contracts, or Roman *foedera*, or bedouin alliances, but this is obviously risky. The form and intention of an alliance are things determined by a particular society at a particular time, and in a different society or a different age these things are bound to be different. This accounts for many of the errors into which scholars have fallen on this point. Interpreters of the past, like courteous travelers, must respect the customs of the country in which they find themselves. But where they have not been told what those customs are, it is not surprising if they commit some blunders.

An even greater difficulty with "covenant" is that it is not necessarily one idea. Recalling again the metaphors cited above, it is plain that they are simple and unitary. There is only one first-fruits law, only one kind of Israelite marriage that we need take into account, and only one kind of reaction is to be expected of a she-bear robbed of her cubs. But we have no right to assume that there was only one kind of arrangement between men which was labeled "covenant." The opposite is much more likely to have been true. For different purposes, we might reason, ancient Israelites must have had different forms and procedures for concluding a binding agreement. It is equally possible that some Israelites thought of a religious covenant based on one legal form, while others, either at the same time or in a different period, cherished the idea of a covenant derived from a different sort of instrument. The rest of this book will be written from the point of view that there were various ways of conceiving of the covenant with God in ancient Israel, centered about two opposite, almost contradictory notions. At this point, of course, this is only a hypothesis, but even now it may be observed that this would account for many of the curious contradictions among scholars who in the late nineteenth and early twentieth century devoted monographs to the covenant. Starting with the assumption that wherever they found the Hebrew word for covenant they were dealing with the same idea, different interpreters achieved remarkably varied views: mutual obligation, we read, is the essence of the relation; the covenant is a completely one-sided arrangement; God initiates any covenant; men take the initiative in concluding it; there are four covenants in the Priestly writer—no, three; no, two. And, of course, in each different work we find the writer struggling with a recalcitrant body of evidence which will not easily fit his scheme. This state of affairs suggests rather strongly that there are tensions and conflicts in the material itself. It is not a case of six blind men and the elephant, but of a group of learned paleontologists creating different monsters from the fossils of six separate species.

So, like Israel of old, we have sent spies ahead into the land, and it promises to be a goodly land, even if there are some giants and other dangers in it. But there are still other preliminaries that must detain us a little longer in the wilderness. We have looked at some of the reasons why "covenant" is a special problem within biblical studies. Now we must face the problems connected with understanding any part of the Old Testament, if only to explain why in succeeding chapters the qualifiers "probably" and "possibly" occur so often. Modern biblical scholars are in the uncomfortable position of knowing more about the Bible and the biblical world than exegetes of earlier ages and of being at the same time much less confident about the nature of Israel's faith and the course of her religious history. To explain how this came about, a brief sketch of the history of biblical interpretation is offered here, at the end of which we will return to our proper concern and see how critical study produced a radical reassessment of the covenant idea. Along with this history, some general information about the Bible is supplied, much of which is essential to our purpose and not all of which is met with somewhere in school.

If we pick up a book titled "An Anthology of English Literature from the Earliest Times to the Present Day" we know about what to expect as far as language is concerned. Even the eighteenth-century bits will seem quaint, the Chaucer will be difficult, and the Beowulf impossible. We would know, too, that nine-tenths of the collection would require us to exercise our imagination and our learning, to put ourselves into the different social and economic world for which it was composed. Even so, it is understandably hard for many to keep this in mind when reading "An Anthology of Hebrew Literature from the Earliest Times to the Close of the Canon." For if we read the Old Testament in the King James version, the language all sounds like the seventeenth century A.D.; or if ours is a modern version, it all sounds contemporary; and if we read the Hebrew, it is apt to seem equally foreign throughout. But a moment's reflection shows that we ought rather to expect a great deal of change in language and style between one of the earliest portions of the Hebrew Bible, the Song of Deborah (Judges 5), from the eleventh century B.C., and the latest work, the book of Daniel, from the second century B.C. Even though biblical Hebrew is to a great extent a literary language, the kind of language that is taught in schools and used for formal composition and does not reflect every shift in popular speech or variety of dialect, the Bible itself provides much evidence for linguistic change over the centuries. "Formerly in Israel, when a man went to inquire of God, he would say, 'Come, let us go to the seer,' because where we say 'prophet' today they used to say 'seer.' " (I Samuel 9:9.) At this point the biblical writer is conscious that usage has changed; at other points it is likely that later writers were not conscious of how literary diction had changed, or did not fully understand the language of an earlier century. Along with this linguistic change went social and economic change, at a pace perhaps less rapid than that experienced today, but nevertheless perceptible. Jeremiah, for instance, living in an age when the institution of monarchy in Israel was four hundred years old, probably had no very precise notion of the role of the *shofetim*, the "Judges" who had led the tribes in the days when there was no king in Israel and every man did what was right in his own eyes. And this remains a problem today, along with many other aspects of the social setting of Israel's literature.

Small parts of the Old Testament are not in Hebrew but in a different Semitic language, Aramaic, and this points to a decisive change in the linguistic situation. Toward the end of the biblical period, especially from the sixth century B.C. on, Aramaic was the tongue used throughout the Near East for international communication and came to be the common spoken language of many Jews. Hebrew came to occupy a secondary position, and although new manuscript finds—the Bar Kokhba letters and other documents from the Judaean desert—show that Hebrew was still used, alongside Aramaic and Greek, for quite ordinary purposes until the second century A.D., after that time Hebrew became "the sacred tongue"—the language of the Bible, of worship, and of scholarship. It was nobody's native tongue.

This explains why translations of the Old Testament begin to be made, even before the last Old Testament book was written (about 165 B.C.) and, of course, before the official canon was agreed on (about A.D. 100). In the last several centuries B.C., Aramaic versions, the Targums, began to be prepared and used. At first these were oral, but later they were committed to writing. Since Alexander and his successors had succeeded in bringing the Greek language and Greek culture to much of the Near East, many Jews grew up with Greek as their mother-tongue, and beginning in the third century B.C., Jewish scholars in Alexandria prepared a Greek translation of the Old Testament, first of the five books of Moses and then of the other books, which came to be called the Septuagint (Latin "seventy"), after the legend that it was produced by seventy scholars.

With the production of these translations we are definitely into the era of biblical interpretation. Although in a sense much of the process of formation of the Old Testament was one of reinterpretation of older traditions, by the last several centuries B.C. certain writings had come to be regarded as Holy Scripture, as a given quantity within the religion. By that time, too, few had access to these writings directly, without the intervention of some kind of interpretation, if only a translation. This will be a good point, then, at which to examine the principles that governed early Jewish exegesis of the Scriptures. Much of what is said on this score will be applicable to early Christian interpretation as well.

Jewish interpreters of the Bible were above all serious, even passionate, about living the life they found commanded there. Their desire was not just to read about Israel, it was to *be* Israel. There was no interest in a remote past for its own sake, but rather "The LORD did not make this covenant with our fathers, but with us, the ones here today, all of us, the living." Beginning after the chastening experience of the exile in Babylon during the sixth century B.C., there was a growing and finally triumphant determination that there should be no more apostasy, no "whoring after other gods," but that every aspect of Jewish life should be brought into submission to the divine law. Denied independent political existence during most periods, Israel was shaped into a community centered about the Scriptures.

The Scriptures, then, must be interpreted to meet the

needs of this community. Quite naturally, there was a desire
for uniformity of interpretation, since a code of conduct does
not admit inner contradictions. This desire for uniformity
had a variety of effects. Certainly it helps account for the
curious history of the text of the Hebrew Bible. Any ancient
book was apt to exist in a variety of forms in its early history.
The author himself, or his pupils, might issue several editions,
often substantially different from one another. Later copy-
ists might carry out extensive revisions: adding material from
elsewhere, rearranging the sections, harmonizing inconsistencies, modernizing the language, and so on. When this
had gone on long enough, various editions of the "same"
book would be noticeably out of harmony with one another.
This natural process affected the Hebrew Scriptures, too, as
has always been clear from the Greek version, the Septuagint,
parts of which were translated from a Hebrew text unlike
that which is known today, and from the Hebrew text of the
Pentateuch preserved by the Samaritans, a sect that broke
away from ordinary Judaism in the last centuries before
Christ. The Dead Sea Scrolls have made it still more evident
that the Hebrew text of the Bible once exhibited a considerable amount of variety. Such variety in text-forms eventually becomes intolerable for any literary work; before long
readers call for a Homer or a Shakespeare that is the same
for everyone. But where the book is Holy Scripture, pressure
is even greater, and the result for the Hebrew Bible was the
choice of one kind of text as authoritative. This edition of
the text, known as the Masoretic text, was well formed
already by the first century A.D., and before long it was
regarded as the only legitimate text for worship and study.
No other kinds were copied. In consequence, until very
recently we have had many hand copies of the Hebrew Bible,
but all of them have agreed so remarkably with one another
that the practical effect was the same as having only one copy.

This achievement of textual uniformity parallels the consistency achieved in rules for the righteous conduct of life. The task of interpretation here was no small one. How to adapt laws originally fitted for little village farming communities to the very different situation in which the Jews of the dispersion found themselves? How deal with apparent inconsistencies in the biblical laws, and how to legislate for situations not obviously or directly dealt with by Moses? Much of early Jewish interpretation is concerned, then, with a search for *halakhah*, the correct principle of conduct for a given situation, arrived at through debate and discussion by the rabbis on the basis of the Bible. In time the decisions of the early rabbis on such matters were themselves codified, written down, and regarded as authoritative, and in turn became the subject of interpretation.

Along with this intensely serious and austere sort of interpretation went another sort that was lighter and directed to a different end, the haggadic. Derived from a word meaning "tale," *haggadah* was homiletic in character, not intended to fix binding religious law, but to exhort, illustrate, edify, and entertain. Often the meaning discovered in a passage is far from its literal sense. The Song of Songs begins: "Kiss me with the kisses of your mouth, for your love is sweeter than wine." [2] Of this the Targum makes the following: "Solomon said: Blessed be the Lord, who has given us the Law, through Moses the great scribe, written on two tables of stone, and the six orders of the Mishnah, and instruction in learning, and who spoke with us face to face like one who kisses his companion out of abounding love, for he loved us more than seventy nations." Although one's first impression of this sort of interpretation is of something uncontrolled, free to hang a tale or a homily on any biblical peg, to

2. This translation smooths over some minor difficulties of person and tense in the Hebrew.

calculate the numerical value of a name and deduce a meaning from it, to make the oddest possible combinations, there is an underlying unity beneath the variety and a common purpose with halakhic interpretation. Haggadic interpretation expresses a different form of the desire for scriptural uniformity: the desire to serve the religious community by showing that the Scriptures are uniformly edifying, that the same message is everywhere if only the interpreter has the art to find it. Even the first line of what seems to be a human love-song yields a message of the love of God and the obligations imposed at Sinai.

Christian interpretation of the Old Testament takes a much different route but ends up at a position not wholly unlike the Jewish one. Jesus read the Scriptures as "they which testify of me," and the New Testament writers carry out the theme that the Old was now fulfilled in the New. This led some Christian thinkers to favor the conclusion that the Christian church could in future dispense with the elder revelation, but the opposite opinion prevailed. Of course, since the movement that had begun within Judaism soon turned to the Greek-speaking Gentiles, the Old Testament of the Christians was the Septuagint, the Greek version. The ensuing loss of contact with the Hebrew meant that for centuries Christian scholars expounded a Greek text, or later a Latin text. A figure such as St. Jerome, who prepared a new Latin translation of the Hebrew text, the so-called Vulgate, in the fifth century, is a very lonely exception indeed. It is depressing to read a genius like Augustine arguing learnedly whether Nimrod was a mighty hunter *before* the Lord, or *against* the Lord, on the basis of the various meanings of the Greek preposition *enantion*, a performance from which the merest smattering of Hebrew would have rescued him (*City of God*, Book XVI, section 4).

With this difference in the linguistic situation, we meet

within Christianity the same devotion to the Scriptures found in Judaism and the same conviction that the whole of Scripture must serve the needs of the religious community for doctrine and edification. Origen is a representative, if somewhat extreme, example of an early Christian approach to the Bible which in modified form became common. Origen, whose works fall in the third century A.D., held that all of Scripture, having God as its author, contains a deep spiritual sense, that the aim of the Bible is to communicate intellectual truths, not history. Anyone who takes that view will very soon meet with lists of "begats" and other homely details not obviously spiritual or intellectual, but Origen is far from embarrassed by such unpromising material. He delights in finding in the Bible such stumbling-blocks, along with things that did not happen and things that could not happen, like days without sun, moon, and stars, or God walking in the garden. They prove his point, that all Scripture has a spiritual meaning, but not all has a literal sense. When Leviticus says that the cereal offering shall be baked in an oven, or fried in a griddle, or cooked in a pan, what sense does it make? How could God care about something like this? Confronted with such absurdities, one must turn to a technique of exegesis used previously by Philo Judaeus for explaining the Old Testament to its cultured despisers and by Greek intellectuals for rendering Homer less offensive: allegory. In this case, the cereal is the Scripture, the oven signifies the heart of man, and the mention of three vessels for baking stands for the multiple senses of Scripture.[3] This principle, that alongside the literal, historical sense of the Bible there were one or more spiritual senses, achieved very widespread acceptance, and though there were those who preferred the

3. Origen's views are found in his *On First Principles*, now conveniently available in the Harper Torchbook edition by G. W. Butterfield with an introduction by Henri de Lubac.

literal sense, they were a minority until the end of the Middle Ages. Both literal and allegorical interpretation were intended to buttress and illustrate the great overarching and all-inclusive system of Christian doctrine and life which was universally believed. Like the Jewish technique that could find Sinai in the Song of Songs, the Christians were able to see the Cross prefigured in the mention of the "woman gathering a couple of sticks" whom Elijah met (you had only to think of her crossing the two sticks). And although the method might seem to have no discipline or bounds at all, the results were controlled by an accumulating body of interpretations accepted as correct and authoritative and by the necessity of conforming to a dogmatic system.

At this point, with due apologies for having drastically oversimplified a complicated process of development, we may survey what had survived of an understanding of ancient Israel. Obviously the religious devotion of Jews and Christians to their holy book had done a great deal to preserve it intact. The Jews had transmitted one variety of Hebrew text with painstaking fidelity, and along with it had begun to produce useful grammatical and lexical works under the stimulus of similar work done by Muslim scholars. A body of traditional exegesis, including the Aramaic Targums, had also been handed down. The Greek translation had flourished in the hands of Christians. Other literary works of antiquity might exist in only a few copies, but there was no lack of manuscripts of the Bible, some of them being very old. In spite of widespread neglect or disdain for the letter, in both camps there was considerable agreement as to much of the historical sense of the Old Testament; the Bible is not all *that* obscure. Of course, throughout this whole discussion I am deliberately disregarding another and very important aspect of the elusive word "understand," the sense in which we would say that a man troubled by his sins "understands" the Fifty-first Psalm better on the basis of a defective translation than the most erudite antiquarian who remains untouched by its contents. On that score who can say how one age compares with another in its understanding of the Bible? We must be content to speak of intellectual grasp of the simple literal sense, but even at this level the picture is not one of unrelieved blackness.

Yet much had been lost, or, more justly stated, much had not yet been discovered. We miss in all this any sense of the past, of how different and strange another age really can be. In the art of the time, perspective had not yet been invented, and all the figures in a scene move on the same plane; so also there was no perception or representation of the depth dividing contemporary life from patriarchs and prophets. And where what the text meant to its first writer and readers was not the first object of concern, resulting glosses were frequently arbitrary and silly. Scripture was a wax nose that could be twisted into any desired shape. The desired shape, it turned out, was all too often something outside the Bible itself, an authoritative code of conduct or system of dogma.

If some of the foregoing was perhaps avoidable, another great loss was inevitable, the loss of any satisfactory knowledge of the ancient world in which Israel had lived and moved. Where few could read Hebrew, there was not one living soul who could read a word of Egyptian or Babylonian or Phoenician. We can be grateful that the Hebrews preserved their ancient history better than any other nation of antiquity. Even so, we should be aware that at the end of the Middle Ages, and for that matter until the nineteenth century, the situation was as described by W. F. Albright: "From the chaos of prehistory the Bible projected as though it were a monstrous fossil, with no contemporary evidence to demonstrate its authenticity and its origin in a human world like ours." [4]

The decisive changes in Christian interpretation had their start in re-acquaintance with the Hebrew Bible, stress on the literal historical sense, and diminished respect for, or outright rejection of, the authority of traditional interpretations and of constituted ecclesiastical authorities in spiritual matters. These tendencies began late in what is usually regarded as the medieval period but found much more public and complete expression in the two-pronged movement of Renaissance and Reformation. Renaissance humanists contributed both directly and indirectly: through a new spirit and through preparation of new editions of the biblical text and grammars and dictionaries of the biblical languages. From that point Christian exegesis was based on the Hebrew text, and Christian Hebraists were able to declare independence of the rabbis and far surpass them in the energy with which they issued grammars and dictionaries. There was a growing tendency to declare independence also of the authority of tradition, a growing ability to read ancient literature rationally and coolly. When Lorenzo Valla, in 1440, published a demonstration that the so-called Donation of Constantine, the basis for papal claims to sovereignty over great portions of Europe, was a forgery, he was not dealing with a biblical question, but the rational, objective method he followed, and his willingness to disagree with authority on a fundamental point, justifies our taking him as a symbol of what humanism would eventually mean for biblical studies. The Reformation was linked with humanism but added other emphases. Luther's motives and those of the other reformers were profoundly religious, but this zeal for God and for reform of his church led in a similar direction: *ad fontes*, to the

4. *Recent Discoveries in Bible Lands* (Pittsburgh, 1955), p. 1.

sources, Scripture against pope or council, "one simple solid sense" against a multiple spiritual sense, and the original languages of the Bible as the basis for study. As it turned out, hardening of the arteries occurred quickly among the followers of the Reformers, and the seventeenth century saw among both Roman Catholics and Protestants more interest in polemics and dogmatics than in working out the implications of a humanistic, critical approach to the Bible.

The fruition began to appear in the *Tractatus Theologico-Politicus* (1670) of Baruch de Spinoza. Although his inclination led him eventually to philosophy, he had as a youth studied to become a rabbi, and both his observations on biblical matters and the rules for interpretation found in this *Tractatus* are almost prophetic in their anticipation of later critical positions. Moses did not write the Pentateuch, which is the work of "someone else, who lived many centuries after Moses," maybe Ezra. The Bible, like any other book, requires no special kind of hermeneutic, but only a rational, historical interpretation. The exegete needs to examine the nature and properties of the language in which the Bible was written; then analyze the subject matter and outline it to show the contents; next study the environment of the books—who wrote them? what do we know of the author's life? what was the occasion for his writing? the age in which he lived? for whom did he write? and in what language?—last, investigate the subsequent history of the book. That, we may say, is nothing remarkable; that is what a careful reader asks about any old book. Which is precisely Spinoza's point: the Bible is to be studied like any old book. It is prophetic, too, that Spinoza, who had earlier been excommunicated from the synagogue in Amsterdam, had his work placed on the church's Index of Prohibited Books. Rational, critical study of the Bible was destined to encounter the hostility of religious conservatives, and much of it would have to be carried on outside the orthodox communities. Another pioneer was Richard Simon, a French Oratorian whose "Critical History of the Old Testament" appeared in 1678. As the title implies, Simon applied a rationalistic, historical approach like that envisioned by Spinoza; once again the Pentateuch received especially close scrutiny: "Moses could not have been the author of all the books attributed to him." Although Simon was regarded as a heretic, and attempts were made to suppress his book, it exercised great influence.

Often in the history of thought, important ideas occur to separate thinkers at about the same time: usually only one is remembered. Thus a certain pastor H. B. Witter published a work on the Pentateuch in 1711 which would have been important if anyone had read it. As it turned out, a professor of medicine and physician of Louis XIV, Jean Astruc, provided the most important key to the composition of the Pentateuch. Astruc had the thoroughly pious intention of explaining how Moses wrote. His title is "Conjectures about the documents which Moses seems to have used to compose the book of Genesis" (1753). The various "memoires" that Moses employed can be distinguished, Astruc said, by the different names of God which occur in various portions. A uses "God" while B uses "Jehovah."

Late in the eighteenth century J. G. Eichorn took over Astruc's criteria for discovering sources in the Pentateuch and added his own: double narratives, characteristic vocabulary of each writer, and so on, and then the Germans of the nineteenth century fell to work along the lines established with characteristic thoroughness and passion. Hypothesis after hypothesis was advanced and debated, and when one hypothesis survived, it could reasonably claim to be the fittest. The Documentary Hypothesis, as widely accepted by scholars toward the end of the nineteenth century, had roughly this shape: The Pentateuch was not written by Moses but is a composite product put together by editors from four documents. The earliest uses the name "Yahweh"; the symbol for this source is "J." [5] Another early source uses the name "God," Hebrew *Elohim*, hence "E." The third document, Deuteronomy ("D"), may be dated most precisely, for it is the basis for the reform undertaken by King Josiah, 621 B.C. Last comes another work using the name "God," *Elohim*, but with a distinctive priestly theology, hence "P"; it comes after the Babylonian exile.

With the work of Julius Wellhausen, whose *Prolegomena to the History of Ancient Israel* (1878) is a watershed in biblical interpretation, we rejoin at last the theme of this book, the covenant, and can measure the radical nature of the revolution that has taken place. Where a naïvely literal reading of the Old Testament had always understood that the covenant with God at Mount Sinai took place in the days of Moses, at the beginning of the history of Israel, with the subsequent story being one of repeated apostasy, chastening, and repentance at the urging of the prophets, we find in Wellhausen's view the idea of a covenant as one of the latest ideas to arise in Israel's history, and a rather minor feature of his presentation. It is not presupposed by the prophets, it grows out of their ideas. Moses was truly a creative figure—Israel's real history begins with him—but the content of Mosaic religion may be summed up in the formula: "Yahweh the God of Israel, and Israel the people of Yahweh." This was not monotheism; it meant much the same as "Chemosh the god of Moab." Yahweh's relation to his people was not defined by a legal bond, for it was a natural one, just as the early cult knew no priesthood with elaborate

5. Since in German, as in older English works, a "J" is used to transliterate a Hebrew y sound, the "J" is derived from the German spelling of Yahwist or Yahwistic.

cultic regulations—no Aaron beside Moses—but was natural and grew out of the life of the people. Yahweh was the protector, the deliverer, and only out of the confrontation with Canaanite religion did it come about that the prophets began to stress the moral and ethical demands of Yahweh and to develop the notion that *only* Yahweh was God. Out of this prophetic interposition of ethical norms between God and his people developed the third state, the legalistic religion of postexilic Judaism.

Covenant? This idea, popular in later times, was not present in early days but was a natural development of the prophets' ethical ideas and of such poetic pictures as Hosea's idea of a marriage between God and Israel. The word "covenant" is rare in the early prophets, and since the developed idea is not yet present—Hosea does not even understand the technical sense—those few passages where it does stand may be suspected of being later additions.

Although Wellhausen made his own contributions to literary criticism, much of his work is based on results achieved through the patient labors of other higher critics. His unique achievement was to have used this material to elaborate the historical synthesis that would be the framework and presupposition for a succeeding generation's work at the Old Testament. It is not too much to say that a critical orthodoxy developed to replace older dogmatic schemes.

Implicit in Wellhausen's work is a view of history as developing, always becoming, always progressing. A number of streams fed this view, the notion of evolution in the biological realm presumably among them, but he seems most directly indebted to Hegel's philosophy of history. Note his three phases: a primitive, natural state, is followed by the prophetic period, its antithesis, which in turn produces its natural consequence, the period of Judaism, the religion of the Law. It is somewhat irrelevant to observe that Wellhausen has no great fondness for the final result; the significant point is that the dogmatic views of an earlier day have not been replaced by a history that is objective and without presuppositions. The controlling assumption throughout is that Israel's history was one of development from a lower, "natural," state to a higher spiritual state.

The twentieth century has seen Wellhausen's reconstruction of Israel's religious pilgrimage challenged from many sides. In many cases the challenge was based on new evidence brought to light through the recovery of the biblical world, and we must now, as one last preliminary, survey the results of the recovery of the ancient Near East, which began in the nineteenth century and reached maturity in the twentieth. Before doing so, however, it is necessary to point out that even if Wellhausen's radical recasting of the biblical record no longer commands widespread assent, this has not brought about a return to the orthodoxy it replaced. Much of the critical dissection of the Bible and redating of the parts has stood the test of time. The bricks have survived the collapse of the building and will have to be used in erecting a replacement.

In telling of the recovery of man's most ancient historical past, I shall leave out the "romance of archaeology," though one could defend the point of view that the "Gee whiz" tone is the proper one in which to write the story. Dull would he be of soul who could yawn at Howard Carter opening the fabulous tomb of King Tut, and duller still he who is not excited by the genius of the great decipherers, Champollion, Grotefend, Rawlinson, and the rest. We must be content to sum up the results. Today, not quite one hundred and fifty years after Champollion's decipherment, a great bulk of Egyptian written material of all sorts, covering roughly the three millennia before our era, can be read with considerable certainty. An even greater quantity of the literature, law, history, hymns, and business papers of ancient Mesopotamia has been discovered through excavation—the bulk is hundreds of times the size of the Hebrew Old Testament—and given this much material, the Akkadian language (a blanket name for various dialects in two main divisions, Babylonian and Assyrian) is in many respects better understood than its cousin, biblical Hebrew. The completely unrelated language that was dominant in Mesopotamia before Akkadian, in the third millennium B.C., Sumerian, can be interpreted with increasing certainty. Our earliest Sumerian literary texts are from about 2600 B.C., over a thousand years before Moses by anyone's chronology. Our own century has seen the decipherment of Hittite, the language of an ancient empire in Asia Minor. The tablets from the ancient Hittite capital now yield a picture of a rich and complex civilization, whereas a previous age knew little about the Hittites beyond the biblical story of Abraham's purchase of a cave from "the sons of Heth." Phoenician has been intelligible since 1837, but this yields in importance to the recovery of another language and literature closely related to Phoenician and to biblical Hebrew· Ugaritic, named after the site of ancient Ugarit, where excavation began in 1929, producing a constant stream of tablets in an alphabetic script that did not long resist decipherment. This is the barest outline and says nothing of the unwritten remains that illuminate and control the picture derived from the texts.

That this new information ought to be of enormous significance for biblical studies is obvious. Take one figure, Abraham, whose father comes from Ur in South Mesopotamia, who lives around Haran in the north, until he sets out on a series of wanderings through Syria-Palestine and even down to Egypt, and who in Palestine deals with Hittites. Now that these places and peoples are no longer so many Xanadus and Skiapodes, we are in a completely different position as interpreters. And now, in dealing with those biblical analogies that hitherto escaped our understanding, like "covenant," there is a chance that we may find the terrestrial side of the equation somewhere in the literature and life of Israel's ancient neighbors.

CHAPTER TWO

THE WORDS OF THE SUN

"Empire" is probably the word we use most in talking about political life in the ancient Near East, and it is apt to convey to our minds the notion of a vast area ruled by an autocratic "Oriental despot." There is a certain justification for this, to be sure, since the course of events did often lead to the formation of an extensive dominion under the control of one central power, and it is also convenient for dividing up ancient history if we can speak of "the Egyptian empire," "the empire of Akkad," and so on. Yet this should not be allowed to make us forget that a more basic, characteristic, and permanent political unit was the city-state. Outside ancient Egypt, the city was the typical unit of political organization. It would be hard for a traveler to miss this point: the mounds covering ancient cities stick up like huge blisters from the Near Eastern landscape, visual reminders that here were the fortresses, the markets, the temples and palaces. To form an idea of the tenacity with which a city might maintain itself, consider Jericho: here the debris from human occupation formed a mound sixty feet high, with the earliest walled city on the site dating to about 7000 B.C. More often than not the individual man owed his political allegiance to a city, and his religious devotion was directed to the gods of a city. According to the laws issued by Hammurapi, if a man commits incest, "they shall make that man leave the city" (Law 154). To be shut out of the city is to be an outlaw, to have no community at all. This sort of tiny unit consisting of one walled town with the fields and unprotected villages that were dependent on it—its "daughters," in biblical terminology—existed much earlier than our earliest written records (about 3000 B.C.) and is the stuff out of which any larger political structure had to be built.

It is not surprising, then, that the need for some sort of order in international, that is, inter-city affairs should be felt very early. As self-sufficient as the city strove to be, there would inevitably be some products it sought outside—stone, tin, copper, salt, or whatever—which forced it into dealings with foreigners. Boundary disputes with neighbors would have to be settled by war or negotiation, and along the great rivers water rights would be a source of inter-city contention. Then too, by about the middle of the third millennium B.C. the idea of empire was already present, one Lugalzaggisi of Umma having seen the advantages to be derived from control over other cities in southern Mesopotamia. From then on rulers sought means of administering the lands of other cities which they had conquered, and smaller powers banded together for resistance to a conqueror or for rebellion against an overlord.

All this produced well-defined forms for the conduct of international affairs. Our evidence is more plentiful for some periods than for others, and the following description is based principally on the situation in the fifteenth through thirteenth centuries B.C., concerning which the archives from El Amarna in Egypt, Ugarit along the North Syrian coast, and Boghaz-köy in Asia Minor provide abundant and detailed information. Many features of this period would apply to earlier and later ages as well. There was much sending and receiving of embassies, and a rather careful distinction between first-class powers and those of lesser importance. The development of highly stereotyped forms of address between rulers permits us to observe this: a superior is "My lord," whereas an equal is "my brother." In writing to a superior or an equal one may well use the approximate equivalent of our

"How are you, I am fine"; to a subordinate it is sufficient to say "I am fine." In some centuries there is one language of international diplomacy, Akkadian, and in those periods scribes whose native tongue was Hittite or Hurrian or Egyptian or a Canaanite dialect write to one another in various sorts of pidgin Akkadian, which was laboriously and badly learned in the local scribal schools. Diplomatic marriages were common. A Babylonian king writes to Amenophis III of Egypt: "You want my daughter for your wife, yet my sister, whom my father gave you, is there with you and no one has seen her of late to say whether she is alive or dead!" The complaint points to the frequency of this device of statecraft, just as in a later period most of Solomon's "seven hundred wives and three hundred concubines" are to be accounted for by his foreign policy.

In this atmosphere of lively, and formal, diplomatic interchange, it was inevitable that there should be fixed forms for concluding alliances. The major problem faced was one of enforcement, which makes it only half-correct to think of ancient treaties as belonging to "international law." In the sphere of law proper, then as now, the community, whether city or tribe, stood ready to enforce breaches of the law and of contracts. "If a man rented a field for cultivation, but has not produced grain in the field, they shall prove that he did not work in the field and he shall give grain to the owner of the field on the basis of those adjoining it" (Laws of Hammurapi, 42). The city depended for its life on the mutual fulfilling of contracts, and so it was ready to force men to keep their word, and it was perfectly able to impose its collective will on an individual citizen. Then as now, no collective force existed for the enforcement of agreements between sovereign political units. A king who could not afford to garrison newly conquered territory might hope that it would not rise in rebellion as soon as he turned his back, and a subject king conspiring with another vassal against an overlord might hope that his partner would show up with ten thousand troops when the day of battle came, but if either were disappointed in his hopes, he had no remedy at law. In the desire to achieve some kind of good faith among nations, to replace a state of constant war by peace, recourse was to the oath, to the gods.

The oath had a subsidiary role in ancient law proper, being reserved for those cases where the community lacked any technique for discovering the truth or for enforcing the right. "If a man's wife was accused by her husband, but was not actually caught lying with another man, she shall make affirmation by god and return to her house" (Laws of Hammurapi, 131). In a doubtful case like this, where there were no witnesses, but only suspicion, the undesirable breach in the marriage could be healed if the woman would swear to her innocence before god, calling down a curse on herself if she should be lying. Some forms of this practice were rather hard on the person concerned, and the oath became an ordeal: the suspected woman in Babylon might have to throw herself into the river, leaving the issue up to the river-god; her counterpart in Israel had to go through an elaborate jealousy ordeal involving drinking a curse upon herself (Numbers 5:11–31). But fundamentally, ancient use of the oath made sense; it filled important gaps in the network of the law.

An ancient treaty, then, is essentially an elaborate oath. There are two fundamental components: the thing to be performed, and the oath, the invoking of divine vengeance in case the promise is not kept. These basic features are discernibly present in extremely early texts, even though the documents are in part obscure or damaged: The famous "Vulture Stele" of Eannatum, a Sumerian text of the twenty-fifth century B.C., contains an oath sworn to him by the city of

Umma; a somewhat later text issued by Entemena of Lagash seems to be another Sumerian treaty; and an Old Elamite version of a treaty between Elam and Naram-Sin of Akkad (twenty-third–twenty-second century B.C.) contains many of the elements found in later treaties. Most of our treaty-texts, however, are later. The classic juristic analysis of their form and intention carried out by Viktor Korošec, to be summarized here, was based on a group of treaties discovered in the archives of the ancient Hittite capital which date to the fifteenth and fourteenth centuries B.C., that is, a century or so before the Israelite conquest of Canaan.

There are six principal parts in the text of a typical treaty: (1) the preamble; (2) the historical prologue; (3) the stipulations; (4) provisions for deposit of the text and for public reading; (5) a list of the divine witnesses to the treaty; (6) blessings and curses. Any single treaty may vary slightly from this outline; the order may be somewhat different, or one of the elements may be omitted. The basic pattern may be discovered in most of them, however, which points to a similarity of underlying concepts. The following example illustrates the intention and form of each part.[1]

1) Preamble: "These are the words of the Sun[2] Mursilis, the great king, the king of the Hatti land, the valiant, the favorite of the Storm-god, the son of Suppiluliumas, the great king, the king of the Hatti land, the valiant."

This, like most of our extant treaties, is not between kings of equal rank, but between one major power and a subordinate kingdom. The term that has become common is "suzerainty treaty," and this word from the language of feu-

1. The translations from Hittite and Akkadian treaty-texts used in this chapter are those of A. Goetze in Ancient Near Eastern Texts Relating to the Old Testament, 2d ed. (Princeton, 1955), pp. 203–6, and are used by permission of the publisher, Princeton University Press.

2. "Sun," or more literally "Sun-god," is the favorite title of the Hittite kings.

dalism fits the situation very well. The preamble already makes clear that the relation is not one of perfect balance. Only Mursilis, the Hittite king, is called "great king," and the pact to follow is granted by him, in his words. In other sorts of texts, royal correspondence, annals, and the like, kings often refer to pacts as "my treaty," or "my oath." "Such-and-such a vassal despised my treaty," they will complain. It is the great king's pact, not in the sense that he is the one expected to obey it but that he is the one who granted it.

2) Historical Prologue (abridged):

Aziras was the grandfather of you, Duppi-Tessub. He rebelled against my father, but submitted again to my father. When the kings of Nuhassi land [a region in Syria] and the kings of Kinza rebelled against my father, Aziras did not rebel. As he was bound by treaty, he remained bound by treaty. As my father fought against his enemies, in the same manner fought Aziras. Aziras remained loyal toward my father and did not incite my father's anger. My father was loyal to Aziras and his country; he did not undertake any unjust action against him or incite his or his country's anger in any way. . . . When my father became god [Hittite idiom for "died"], and I seated myself on the throne of my father, Aziras behaved toward me just as he had behaved toward my father. It happened that the Nuhassi kings and the king of Kinza rebelled a second time against me. But Aziras, your grandfather, and DU-Tessub [correct pronunciation of the first part of this name is unknown], your father, (did not take their side); they remained loyal to me as their lord. (When he grew too old) and could no longer go to war and fight, DU-Tessub fought against the enemy with the foot soldiers and the charioteers of the Amurru land [Amurru, Duppi-Tessub's state, was also in North Syria] just as he had fought with foot soldiers and charioteers against the enemy. And the Sun destroyed them.

[Gap in the text]

When your father died, in accordance with your father's word I did not drop you. Since your father had mentioned to me your name, I sought after you. To be sure, you were sick and ailing, but although you were ailing, I, the Sun, put you in the place of your father and took your brothers (and) sisters and the Amurru land in oath for you.

Here is history told from a very particular point of view. It concerns only the relationship of the Hittite state to the vassal, Amurru. Any other nations come in only incidentally, and internal affairs in either land have no importance. What is important is, in the first place, the behavior of the ruling house of Amurru as vassals, which means primarily military allies. Here the history reaches back to the grandfather of the reigning monarch, and in general these historical prologues do not begin much before the first treaty between the nations in question. In this case, Aziras, the grandfather, had at first been disloyal but later proved a good ally, as did DU-Tessup, the father. The second point stressed is the kindness of the overlord. Mursilis has heeded DU-Tessup's wish and placed his chosen son, Duppi-Tessub, on the throne, even though he was weak and sickly—no small favor with ambitious brothers on the scene.

It is evident from even one example that this historical prologue, though a recurring feature of the treaties, could not be stereotyped. It tells a story fitted to the particular partners involved. The treaty form was not a standard contract form in which you needed only to fill in the proper names and sign on the line. The history had a function to perform: it was meant to place the relation on a basis other than that of sheer force. True, the Hittite king had bigger armies than Duppi-Tessub, and at some time in the past his father had presumably beaten Amurru on the field of battle, and Mursilis was able to do the same. But why should it come to that? Your fathers served Hatti, and it was well with them, and you, Duppi-Tessub, owe your throne to me. This history is the basis for your obligation. Parenthetically, if the history were to create any sense of obligation, it had to be substantially accurate.

Another feature of treaty practice is implicit in this history. Conclusion of a new treaty takes place just after the accession of a new vassal-king. The intent throughout is that the alliance should be permanent; a later clause will make it explicit: "You, Duppi-Tessub, remain loyal toward the king of the Hatti land, the Hatti land, my sons (and) my grandsons forever!" Yet since the death of the monarch who had actually sworn fealty might raise some question as to whether the next generation was bound by his oath, the accession of a new king was the signal for a reaffirmation or renegotiation of his father's treaties.

3) Stipulations (abridged):

When I, the Sun, sought after you in accordance with your father's word, and put you in your father's place, I took you in oath for the king of the Hatti land, the Hatti land, and for my sons and grandsons. So honor the oath to the king and the king's *kin!* And I, the king, will be loyal toward you, Duppi-Tessub. When you take a wife, and when you beget an heir, he shall be king in the Amurru land likewise. And just as I shall be loyal toward you, even so shall I be loyal toward your son. But you, Duppi-Tessub, remain loyal toward the king of the Hatti land, the Hatti land, my sons (and) my grandsons forever! The tribute which was imposed upon your grandfather and your father—they presented 300 shekels of good, refined first-class gold weighed with standard weights—you shall present them likewise. Do not turn your eyes to anyone else! Your fathers presented tribute to Egypt; you (shall not do that!)
[Gap in the text; those portions of the following enclosed in brackets are restored from other treaties.]
[With my friend you shall be friend, and with my enemy you shall be enemy. If the king of the Hatti land is either in the Hurri land, or in the land of Egypt, or in the country of Astata, or in the country of Alse—any country contiguous to the territory of your country that is friendly with the king of the Hatti land—(some others are listed) but turns around and becomes inimical toward the king of the Hatti land while the king of the Hatti land is on a marauding campaign—if then you, Duppi-Tessub, do not remain loyal together with your foot soldiers and your charioteers and if you do not fight

wholeheartedly; or if I should send out a prince (or) a high
officer with foot soldiers and charioteers to reinforce you,
Duppi-Tessub (for the purpose of) going out to maraud in
an]other c[ountry—if then you, Duppi-Tessub, do not fight
wholehea]rtedly (that) enemy with [your army and your
charioteers] and speak as follows: "I am under an oath of
loyalty, but [how am I to know] whether they will beat the
enemy, or the enemy will beat them?" or if you even send
a man to that enemy and inform him as follows: "An army
and charioteers of the Hatti land are on their way; be on your
guard!"—(if you do such things) you act in disregard of your
oath. . . .

[After further clauses concerning military aid] If anyone
of the deportees from the Nuhassi land or of the deportees
from the country of Kinza whom my father removed and myself removed escapes and comes to you, (if) you do not seize
him and turn him back to the king of the Hatti land, and
even tell him as follows: "Go! Where you are going to, I do
not want to know," you act in disregard of your oath.

If anyone utters words unfriendly toward the king of the
Hatti land before you, Duppi-Tessub, you shall not withhold
his name from the king. . . . Or if the king of the Hatti
land is getting the better of a country and puts them to flight,
and they come to your country, if then you desire to take
anything from them, ask the king of the Hatti land for it!
You shall not take it on your own! If you lay hand on it by
yourself or conceal it, (you act in disregard of the oath).

This is a mere sampling of the obligations laid on vassals
in these treaties, but a fair sampling, because in this part of
the treaty less variety is found than in the historical intro-
ductions. The essential obligation laid on the vassal is that of
loyalty, that is, that he shall have no independent foreign
policy. "Do not turn your eyes to anyone else!" is the command, or as it is succinctly expressed in another passage:
"With my friend you shall be friend, and with my enemies
you shall be enemy." The chief test of loyalty will come in
time of war. Duppi-Tessub must then fight "wholeheartedly"
(literally, "with all your heart"), and this is spelled out in
very practical terms and at some length. Since there were dis-
sident elements within the Hatti land, it was to be expected

that from time to time some potential rebel might flee and seek refuge in Amurru or at least safe-conduct through the state. But Duppi-Tessub is obligated by his oath to arrest and extradite all such, and this is a very common clause in the treaties. It goes without saying that a vassal must not speak against his lord, but beyond that, he must also report any unfriendly talk that he hears. The vassal is not to play jackal to the overlord's lion; if a beaten enemy falls into his hands, the spoil belongs to the great king, and if the vassal wants anything, he must ask.

Note also the style here. This is not the austere formalism of a collection of laws like that of Hammurapi, where the formulation is as general and impersonal as possible, each law containing condition and consequence: "If a man . . . , then. . . ." Most of the treaty stipulations have the form of conditional sentences ("If you do such-and-such, you act in disregard of your oath"), but the use of the second person and first person ("I shall be loyal toward you") imparts a vividness and directness lacking in the laws. There is an occasional straightforward command: "Do not! . . . You shall not!" And note a further difference from the law in the statement of penalty. In a legal statement the penalty is explicit, whether death, a fine, or some other form of punishment; here, in the event of disloyalty, "you act in disregard of the oath" is all that can be said. The statement of penalty is left for other parts of the treaty.

But what about the overlord's obligations? There are none, at least none definite enough to be compared to those laid on the vassal. To be sure, the historical introduction stresses the good record of Hittite kings and the good intentions of the reigning monarch: "My father was loyal to Aziras and his country; he did not undertake any unjust action against him." "I, the king, will be loyal to you, Duppi-Tessub," says Mursilis, and goes on to promise that he will see to it that Duppi-Tessub's son succeeds to his father's throne without any troubles. Except for this sort of very general assurance of decent treatment of the vassal, the overlord does not promise a thing, and this is an important point. As we shall see later, he, the Hittite king, does not take any oath, and the curses for breach of treaty are all invoked upon the vassal. The Hittite king intends to behave in an upright way, but he will not, so to speak, put it in writing, and there is no chance of taking him to court before the gods if he offends the vassal king.

4) Provisions for Deposit of the Text and for Public Reading. Since this common feature is by chance missing from the treaty quoted here, a specimen will be cited from a different pact, that between Mursilis' grandfather, Suppiluliumas, and Mattiwaza of Mitanni, a kingdom on the North Euphrates: "A duplicate of this tablet has been deposited before the Sun-goddess of Arinna, because the Sun-goddess of Arinna regulates kingship and queenship. In the Mitanni land (a duplicate) has been deposited before Tessub, the lord of the *kurinnu* [a kind of shrine] of Kahat. At regular *intervals* shall they read it in the presence of the king of the Mitanni land and in the presence of the sons of the Hurri country."

The treaty is put in the most sacred shrines of the chief gods of the two lands involved, for an obvious purpose: so that the gods could read it and be reminded from time to time of the provisions of the oath sworn in their presence. The Sun-goddess of Arinna stands at the head of the Hittite pantheon as far as these matters are concerned, and Tessub (also spelled Teshub) is the great storm-god and most powerful deity of the Mitannian state. But men also should remember the oath, so it is stipulated that each year someone should read the text to the vassal-king and his nobles. Implicit in this command is the idea that the treaty should be in a language the sworn parties could understand, and there is direct evidence for this in the case of the famous treaty between the Hittite king Hattusilis III and Rameses the Great of Egypt. A copy in the international language, Akkadian, has been found in the excavations at the old Hittite capital, and a version in the Egyptian language, still extant, was carved on the walls of the temple of Amon at Karnak and on the mortuary temple of Rameses at Thebes.

5) Divine Witnesses to the Treaty. Since the Mursilis-Duppi-Tessub treaty is badly broken at this point, the following discussion is again based on the Suppiluliumas-Mattiwaza pact:

> At the conclusion of this treaty we have called the gods to be assembled and the gods of the contracting parties to be present, to listen and to serve as witnesses: The Sun-goddess of Arinna who regulates kingship and queenship in the Hatti land, the Sun-god, the lord of heaven, the Storm-god, the lord of the Hatti land, Seris and Hurris, the mountains Nanni and Hazzi . . . [over fifty names of other gods follow], all the gods and goddesses of the Hatti land, the gods and goddesses of the country of Kizzuwatna, the former gods, Nara, Namsara, Minku, Amminku, Tussi, Ammizadu, Alalu, Anu, Antu, Ellil, Ninlil, Bēlat-Ekalli, the mountains, the rivers, the Tigris (and) the Euphrates, heaven and earth, the winds (and) the clouds;
>
> Tessub, the lord of heaven and earth, Kusuh and Simigi, the Harranian Moon-god of heaven and earth, Tessub, lord of the *kurinnu* of Kahat, etc. [about twenty-five more deities].

By now the reader may feel that he has left the realm of the rational and is up against sheer mumbo-jumbo. Actually, although many of these barbarous names elude the understanding of scholars as well, most of them are known to some extent from other texts, and there are some definable underlying principles involved in the compilation of these lists of divine witnesses. The list begins with the gods of the land of the overlord, given in abridged form in the first paragraph above. Since the population of the Hatti land was extremely mixed, and since the ruling class was both tolerant of old cults and hospitable to new ones, the list of Hittite gods is very long, the most important deities being placed first. The intention is that the overlord's gods should be aware of the vassal's oath, especially in case he should break it, when they as the most powerful of all gods would be expected to wreak vengeance.

The second paragraph above contains some of the deities of the vassal. His gods are called on too, so that he will have no hiding place if he ever breaks his word. Thus the profusion of gods actually expresses very simple ideas, and the length of the list is occasioned, not by any murky desire to heap up meaningless words, but by the same motive that leads modern lawyers to write "give, bequeath, and assign"—all loopholes must be covered.

At the end of the list of gods of the Hittites stands a series that calls for special mention: the list of "former gods" followed by "the mountains, the rivers, the Tigris and Euphrates, heaven and earth, the winds (and) the clouds." This has called forth a good deal of discussion among biblical scholars because in the Bible mountains and hills, heaven and earth, are occasionally summoned to be witnesses to God's controversy with his people. This topic will be dealt with in chapter six.

6) Blessings and Curses [cited from the Mursilis-Duppi-Tessub treaty]:

> The words of the treaty and the oath that are inscribed on this tablet—should Duppi-Tessub not honor these words of the treaty and the oath, may these gods of the oath destroy Duppi-Tessub together with his person, his wife, his son, his grandson, his house, his land and together with everything that he owns.
>
> But if Duppi-Tessub honors these words of the treaty and the oath that are inscribed on this tablet, may these gods of the oath protect him together with his person, his wife, his son, his grandson, his house (and) his country.

This is the most common form in which the sanctions for breaking the oath and the benefits of keeping it are couched, as far as the second-millennium Hittite treaties are concerned. The curses aim at total destruction of the offender, all he is and all he has. The lawyer's language is heard again: "Duppi-Tessub, together with his person" is cursed—there is to be no mental reservation, no casuistic wriggling-out through a psychology that sees a man and his "person" or "soul" as separate entities. In a different formulation some jurist foresees that a man might try to escape the curse on his wife and children by taking a second wife after the oath was sworn, so a curse is pronounced to cover that contingency as well. The curse is not limited to the vassal king but is spread, in widening circles, over his wife and children, to the third generation, his possessions and his country. This reminds us again that we are in a different world from that of ancient law. In law, whether in Mesopotamia or Israel or elsewhere, the penalty for a man's wrongdoing was inflicted on his own person, with very few exceptions, and the punishment fit the crime. The *lex talionis* (law of retaliation), "an eye for an eye" and the rest of it, was intended to limit the damages exacted to the extent of the injury done. But punishment for breach of this oath by the gods is neither limited or proportionate. It is proportionate only to the powers offended, the great gods, not to the extent of actual damage done. In the treaty cited above the blessing is the mirror-image of the curse, but, considering all our extant treaties, this is not normally the case. Especially in later treaties, curses predominate, which is not surprising. They are the most effective guarantee that the oath will be kept. No one will refrain from rebellion just because he does not want to miss some future divine blessings; he may refrain if he is terrified at the thought of the curse of the gods.

Treaties from the first millennium B.C. have, as a rule, much more elaborate lists of curses, cast in the most lurid and picturesque terms, and these will engage our attention when we take up their biblical counterparts. There is one Hittite treaty that rises above the rather perfunctory curse cited here; one sentence must be quoted for the sake of the topic that closes this chapter. "May the oaths sworn in the presence of these gods break you like reeds."

As full and as clear as these documents are, they do not tell the full story about ancient treaty-making. The text itself is only the abstract record of the agreement and for the most part leaves out of account any negotiations that may have preceded the treaty, the actual ceremonies by which the oath was sworn, and any practices associated with keeping the treaty in force or proceedings against a rebellious vassal. These aspects have to be pieced together out of other sorts of materials for the most part, and on some matters we have little information. The kind of events that might precede the making of a treaty are vividly depicted in the following story of how Ahab of Israel dealt with a conquered enemy, Ben Hadad of Damascus (I Kings 20.31–35): "Then his courtiers [Ben Hadad's] said to him, 'Here, now, we have heard that the kings of Beth Israel are merciful kings. Let us put sackcloth about our loins and ropes on our heads and go out to the king of Israel. Maybe he will spare your life.' So they put sackcloth about their loins and ropes on their heads and came to the king of Israel. They said: 'Your servant [note the technical term for a vassal], Ben Hadad, says: Let me live.' He [Ahab] said: 'Is he still alive? He is my brother [technical term for a partner in a treaty between equals].' . . ." Later Ben Hadad says, " 'The cities which my father took from your father I will return . . . but as for me, let me off with a treaty.' So he [Ahab] made a treaty with him and let him go."

The actual ceremony of swearing to a covenant took numerous forms. We hear of treaties sworn by eating together, by oil and water, by drinking from a cup, by "puppy and lettuce," and so on. Not all these acts meant exactly the same thing. There is a case in which the representative of the king of Mari, an important city on the mid-Euphrates in the early second millennium, called on to function at a covenant-making ceremony, refuses to have it sworn by "puppy and lettuce" and instead insists that the ceremony used be the more common one of killing a young donkey.[3] Even if some of the more esoteric details escape us, it is clear that the acts associated with conclusion of a treaty generally have to do with some sort of curse. They are the counterparts in dramatic action of the written maledictions. Treaty "by oil and water" evidently involved smearing oil on the skin and drinking water, to introduce the curse into the very body of the swearer: "Let (the curse) enter like water into his innards, and like oil into his bones," as one of the imprecatory psalms puts it (109:18). Hosea refers contemptuously to the same practice: "They make a covenant with Assyria, and smear on oil for Egypt" (12:2); and Jeremiah complains: "Now why would you go to Egypt, to drink the waters of the Nile or why would you go to Assyria to drink the waters of the Euphrates?" (2:18).[4]

The most widely attested form of swearing to a covenant, however, involved cutting up an animal. The man

3. For the incident mentioned here and for further discussion of "puppy and lettuce" and some other forms of swearing, see the study by George Mendenhall, "Puppy and Lettuce in Northwest Semitic Covenant Making," *Bulletin of the American Schools of Oriental Research*, 133 (February, 1954): 26–30.

4. On covenant by oil and water, see the study by K. Veenhof in his review of Ernst Kutsch, *Salbung als Rechtsakt*, *Bibliotheca Orientalis*, 23 (1966): 308–13, with references to earlier treatments by McCarthy and Deller.

taking the oath is identified with the slaughtered animal. "Just as this calf is cut up, so may Matiel be cut up," is the way it is put in the text of an Aramaic treaty from the eighth century B.C., and an earlier document describes a similar ceremony: "Abba-AN swore to Yarim-Lim the oath of the gods, and cut the neck of a lamb, (saying): 'If I take back what I gave you. . . .'" The consequence is not expressed and does not need to be. Abba-AN may have drawn his finger across his throat, or it may have been sufficient to point to the slain lamb. Among the Israelites it seems that a common way of identifying the parties to a covenant with the victim was to cut up the animal and pass between the parts. Jeremiah tells us that this is how king Zedekiah of Judah and his nobles made an agreement between them to free their Hebrew slaves, and we can see with especial clarity that this cutting-up of a calf had the effect, in their conception, of putting them under a curse. For when they, in a very short time, broke their word, Jeremiah announces God's judgment: "I will make the men who transgressed my covenant, who did not carry out the provisions of the covenant which they concluded before me, (like) the calf which they cut in two and passed between its parts" (34:18). They had asked for it. From this ceremony is derived the Hebrew idiom for making a treaty, *karat berit*, "to cut a treaty." The same idiom occurs in other languages, notably in Greek, where Homer's phrase is *horkia tamnein*, literally, "to cut oaths."

Of course, the treaty which had been drawn up with such care and ratified with such awful solemnities could be broken casually and unceremoniously. Spring was, in the biblical phrase, "the time when kings go forth," and at times it seems as though the previous summer's covenants had been intended only to tide the nations over the winter. Yet there are exceptions, and one case in particular demonstrates that the fear of the gods was enough to move a great state to keep its oath to another. A great plague had struck the land of the Hittites. For twenty years it had been claiming its victims, and King Mursilis and his people knew that the gods were displeased. We learn of Mursilis' search for the reason in a long prayer that is intrinsically interesting as a specimen of what piety could be in those days, being a blend of legal calculation, evidently sincere humility ("It is only too true that man is sinful"), and trust ("The bird takes refuge in its nest, and the nest saves its life"). But for our purpose the most striking feature is the answer Mursilis gets, from an oracle, as to the cause of the plague. There are two ancient tablets, he is told, and on consulting them he discovers from one that the offerings to a deified river had been neglected and from the other, that a treaty with Egypt sworn before the storm-god had been broken in the days of his father. His father had attacked Egyptian holdings in Syria and had brought prisoners back with him, and they had introduced the plague. Now the sin of the father had been visited on the son, who does not complain; that is, after all, what the oath specifies. But he makes what restitution he can, after all these years, sends prisoners home, and asks for forgiveness.[5] In sum, any king might break his sworn word when the occasion offered, but the religious climate was such that any subsequent disaster—a plague, a defeat, or the like—might be regarded as the curse being worked out on him and his people.

Perceptive readers will already begin to sense something familiar in all this or anticipate the arguments to follow, and they may be anxious to get on with the proper subject

5. The full text of this prayer is found in a translation by A. Goetze in *Ancient Near Eastern Texts Relating to the Old Testament*, pp. 394–96. Princeton University Press.

of this book, the covenants between God and Israel. But study of one more passage seems worth a slight delay. It is a biblical passage, a portion of Isaiah 36, but has nothing directly to do with Israel's faith. Quite the contrary, it is the speech of an Assyrian high official who has been sent down by Sennacherib to call for the surrender of Jerusalem on the famous occasion when "the Assyrian came down like a wolf on the fold." It is a long speech but is included here to show how an understanding of ancient international treaties can bring to life a single biblical chapter and, thereby, of course, how thoroughly Israel was involved in this whole world of embassies and alliances, divine witnesses and curses.

When three high officials of King Hezekiah come out to parley with the Rabshakeh—Chief Cupbearer of the Assyrian king—he delivers the following in a loud voice, just outside the walls of Jerusalem:

> Say to Hezekiah: Thus says the great king, the king of Assyria: "What is it that you are trusting in? Do you think that planning and power to make war are a matter of mere talk? Now, in whom have you put your trust, that you have rebelled against me? You have put your trust in that broken reed Egypt—if a man leans on it it will go into his palm and pierce it, and that is how Pharaoh king of Egypt is to all who rely on him! And if you say, 'We trust in Yahweh, our God' . . . Now, did I invade this land so as to destroy it, in defiance of Yahweh? It was Yahweh who commanded me: 'Invade this land and destroy it.'"
>
> Then Eliakim and Shebna and Joah said to the Rabshakeh: "Please, speak to your servants in Aramaic, for we understand it, but don't speak to us in Hebrew in the hearing of the people who are on the wall." But the Rabshakeh said: "Was it to your lord and to you that my lord sent me to say these things? No, but to the men who are sitting on the wall, who will have to eat their own excrement and drink their own urine along with you." So the Rabshakeh stood and cried out with a loud voice in Hebrew: "Listen to the words of the great king, the king of Assyria" (Isaiah 36:4–13).

Woven into this speech are the terms and concepts surveyed in this chapter—the king of Assyria is "great king," and before his emissary the Judaean officials use a deferential mode of referring to themselves: "your servants." "Trust" figures very prominently in the speech, for if the Jews have refused to trust their proper sovereign they must be trusting something else. The word "trust" is used over and over in just this way in Assyrian royal inscriptions. The Rabshakeh claims that Yahweh has sent him—and we can see that this is far from preposterous. Israel had sworn loyalty to Assyria before Yahweh; this justifies Sennacherib's invasion and makes their cause hopeless.[6] Legally at least, the Rabshakeh has an unbeatable case, and in a later age Ezekiel would have agreed, interestingly enough. The Jewish representatives call for use of the current international language, Aramaic, but the Assyrian insists on using their native tongue, Hebrew, and they shudder, for he is reminding the people on the wall of the curses they were bringing on themselves by this rebellion. There may be an allusion to the sort of curse mentioned above: "May the oaths . . . break you like reeds." Pharaoh had sworn to supply Israel with horses and chariots, but where are they? Pharaoh does not keep his promises and is a "broken reed." [7] The coarse threat that the Rabshakeh shouts to the people on the wall is probably more than an exaggerated description of what they might come to in the ensuing siege, for there is a parallel in the curses attached to two Assyrian treaties, one of them

6. This understanding of the verse was suggested by M. Tsevat, "The Neo-Assyrian and Neo-Babylonian Vassal Oaths and the Prophet Ezekiel," *Journal of Biblical Literature*, 78 (1959): 199–204, for reasons that seem convincing to me. For a divergent opinion and a good example of a "form-critical" treatment of an Old Testament passage, see Brevard S. Childs, *Isaiah and the Assyrian Crisis*, Studies in Biblical Theology, 2d ser., no. 3 (Naperville, Ill., 1967), especially pp. 76–93.
7. I owe this suggestion to my former colleague Herbert Huffmon.

written about fifty years before the incident at Jerusalem: "May tar and pitch be your food, may the urine of an ass be your drink." It is unlikely that Isaiah gives an exact stenographic account of the words spoken on this occasion. No doubt Hebrew historians, like Greek historians, sometimes composed appropriate speeches for their characters to deliver, and this chapter may give us, not what was said, but what ought to have been said, what was typical or appropriate. Even so, it permits us to conclude that the Israelites were thoroughly, even uncomfortably, familiar with what a treaty involved.

CHAPTER THREE

SINAI AND SHECHEM

What is said casually in the Bible is often more significant than what is stressed. For this reason Joshua 8:34 is particularly interesting: "Then afterward he [Joshua] read all the words of the law, the blessing and the curse, just as it all was written in the book of the law." Our analysis of treaty-texts has made it clear that blessing and curse forms a standard, even essential, part of ancient covenants, and here we find a verse that puts blessing and curse together with Israelite law, and quite offhandedly, leaving the impression that this association was common knowledge, a thing that required no explanation.

This sample may serve a double purpose. It should encourage us to think that a search of the Bible for parallels to treaty-texts will be rewarding. But it also presents in miniature the major problem involved. If one had only to take the treaties and lay them down next to copies of biblical covenants, it would be easy enough to discover resemblances and differences. But in this case we are not given, in so many words, the text of any of Israel's treaties with God. What we do have within the scriptures are various accounts of what happened when a covenant was made, or renewed, or broken, or stories of how people lived under this bond tying them to God and to one another. It is very much like comparing the rules for a game with the way we see a group of players performing. If the rules are indeed for the game we are watching, there will be a correspondence. By observing closely and long enough one could deduce the rules that the players are following, or given the rules, one could predict something of the shape that an actual game might take, and yet the correspondence will not be perfect. There will be features of play not anticipated in the rules—the knuckleball or T-formation, for instance—and rules, like the infield fly rule, that need not be invoked very often. The exercise of understanding and imagination would be required, and this is true also of our undertaking, for most often we will find in the Bible the players and the game, not the formal statement of the rules. This is true also of the two main passages to be examined here, Exodus 20, which deals with Sinai, and Joshua 24, which tells of a covenant at Shechem. Even though these resemble formal texts of covenants at some points, they are most exactly described as narratives of how a treaty with God was made.

One other preliminary needs to be clearly understood before we can undertake our point-for-point comparison. Even though it seems appropriate to call this chapter "Sinai and Shechem," this must not be taken to mean that the two chapters to be discussed in detail, Exodus 20 and Joshua 24, give us eyewitness accounts of what happened. The Exodus materials treated here would be assigned by most to "J" and "E" (the Yahwistic and Elohistic documents) and so would be no later than about the eighth century B.C. Joshua 24 would also be considered by most to be at least as ancient. Even so, this is a long way from the time of Moses or Joshua; in their present form our documents are centuries later than the events and words they purport to relate. This dictates the procedure followed here. The question of the antiquity of the ideas discovered in Exodus and Joshua will be left until later. We are initially concerned only with establishing what was believed to have happened at Sinai, or Shechem, by some persons within Israel at some unspecified time. I say "some persons" because here too we must speak by the card, especially about

Sinai. Aside from the "J" and "E" materials taken up here, there is an account of what happened at Sinai by the Priestly writer ("P"), a retrospective account by the Deuteronomist ("D"), and other evidence as well which would have to be drawn in if a full account of how Israel understood the Sinai event were being attempted. We are taking up only a fair-sized slice of the available biblical material, and as frustrating as it may be to be fenced off from the sacred mountain by critical principles, it is best to be clear about the limitations imposed by our material. With this in mind, we may now set about considering such parallels as exist between treaties and biblical covenants, following the lead of George Mendenhall, who was the first to call attention to the resemblances.[1]

Exodus 20

Then God spoke all these words:
"I am Yahweh your God,
Who brought you out of the land of Egypt, out of the house of bondage.
You shall not have other gods besides me.
You shall not make yourself a graven image, or a likeness of anything in heaven above or in the earth beneath, or in the water under the earth. You shall not bow down to them or serve them.
For I, Yahweh your God, am a jealous God, one who brings the iniquity of fathers upon their children even to the third and fourth generation for those who hate me, and one who keeps faith unto thousands of generations with those who love me and keep my commandments.
You shall not swear falsely by the name of Yahweh, your God, for Yahweh will not acquit anyone who swears falsely by his name.
Remember the Sabbath, so as to keep it holy. Six days you shall labor, and do all your work, but the seventh day is a day of rest belonging to Yahweh your God. You shall not do any work, you or your son, or your daughter or your slaves, male or female, or your cattle or the alien who lives among

1. Reference to Professor Mendenhall's works on the covenant will be found among the Suggestions for Further Reading.

you, because Yahweh made heaven and earth, the sea, and everything in them in six days, and on the seventh day he rested. Therefore Yahweh blessed the seventh day and made it holy.

Honor your father and your mother, so that your days may be long in the land Yahweh your God is going to give you. You shall not commit murder. You shall not commit adultery. You shall not steal. You shall not give false testimony against your neighbor. You shall not covet another man's house. You shall not covet another man's wife, or his slave, male or female, or his ox or his donkey or anything that belongs to someone else."

If we compare this with a suzerainty treaty, remembering that the Hebrews use the same word for this pact with God, *berit*, as they do for treaties between kings, we see at the outset that there is at least an essential similarity in the status of the partners. The relation that is formalized is a lopsided one, the two parties being by no means equal in strength or status. It is not thereby a mere edict. Neither party, not even the "vassal" Israel, is purely passive. But the roles are very different. The treaty is not negotiated. The suzerain, or God, simply offers his terms. The vassal's (Israel's) share is to decide whether this is for him, and if so, to swear. (Whether this last element is present in our Sinai narrative will be taken up later in this chapter.)

Turning to specific formal features, we can identify here, without much difficulty, a counterpart to the prologue of the treaty in "I am Yahweh, your God." It is briefer than the titulary of the Hittite king, but not less impressive.

Finding a historical introduction is a little more problematic. We do have, standing in the proper place, "Who brought you out of the land of Egypt," and so on. Does this count? It is brief, but one might say that it is nevertheless as long as Yahweh's dealings with Israel. As in a Hittite treaty, this is history from a very particular point of view: the story of the relation of two parties, told to justify the treaty now proposed, and Yahweh's dealings with Israel begin with the exodus. Some might well ask, "How about Abraham, Isaac, and Jacob?" and later we will have to look for a reason why they are not part of the statement made here. All the same, a more important question would be: Does this history, the exodus, function in the same way that treaty-history was intended to function? Is it regarded in the Old Testament as the basis for Israel's obligation to God? These questions are really rhetorical. Of course the exodus was understood that way, and this means that we are on safe ground in thinking that its presence here constitutes a genuine parallel to the international legal form.

The Ten Commandments constitute an obvious parallel to the stipulations of the suzerainty treaty. Our familiarity with the Commandments makes it a bit strange, perhaps, to think of them in this light, but the basic likeness is there. To have one lord is the principal comand in the treaty, and this is the basic demand of the First Commandment also. In treaties, outside of the requirement that the vassal should have but one suzerain, and the positive demands made on him for military assistance and yearly tribute, not much is said about the conduct of affairs in the vassal's own state. This corresponds to the casting of the Commandments in negative form, as Mendenhall has pointed out. Certain acts are intolerable if there is to be any covenant with God, or any life together as his people—murder, theft, adultery, perjury, and so on—but once these forbidden areas have been fenced off, the rest of their affairs are for them to manage. We come the closest to the spirit of the Ten Commandments in a series of treaties which a Hittite king made with three separate vassals in identical terms, that is, the situation is one where the monarch has not just one, but several of his servants in mind. "Behold, within my land are three noblemen: you, O Targashnallis, Mashhuiluwas, and Manappa-Dattas. . . . The one of you is not to fall out with the other, and one should not seek to kill the other, or capture the other. And if you, Targashnallis, do evil against them, I will take their part, and you will be my enemy. But if they fall out with you, then I will take your part, and they shall be my enemies. [And] because I gave [you] the same pact, be at one [among yourselves], just as you have the same pact. . . ." [2] The relation of these three is henceforth to be determined by their common obligation to the Hittite king. The same conviction is implicit in the Commandments: each Israelite has certain obligations toward other Israelites which stem from their common allegiance to God. Note also the apodictic formulation, that is, that the Commandments are not cast in an "If . . . , then . . ." pattern, but are direct commands: "You shall . . . you shall not." This way of expressing commands is relatively rare in Near Eastern law but, as stated above, is found in the terms of treaties.[3] Such stylistic features are not to be over-stressed, and by themselves mean relatively little. But when we have, as is true here, a similar setting and an essential similarity of ideas, we are perhaps justified in regarding the common details of style as significant too.

2. The English translation of these lines is based on Johannes Friedrich's German rendering of the Hittite. See his "Staatsverträge des Hatti-Reiches in hethitischer Sprache," Part 1, *Mitteilungen der Vorderasiatisch-Aegyptischen Gesellschaft*, 31 (1926), 61 (treaty of Mursilis II with Targashnallis, reverse, ll. 2–10).

3. The importance of these differences in formulation was first pointed out in 1934 by Albrecht Alt in a classic study now happily available in English translation, "The Origins of Israelite Law," *Essays on Old Testament History and Religion*, trans. R. A. Wilson (Oxford, 1966), pp. 79–132. The reader will find information on subsequent studies in this field in Mendenhall's *Law and Covenant* and in the other works listed in the article by Walter Harrelson, "Law in the Old Testament," *Interpreter's Dictionary of the Bible* (New York and Nashville, 1962).

Note also that there is no formal obligation on Yahweh's part, just as the Hittite king did not swear to perform anything in a treaty with a vassal. Yahweh's good will is implicit; he is the one who has graciously brought them out of the house of bondage. He will continue to be loyal and kind, since he is "One who keeps faith unto thousands of generations with those who love me and keep my commandments." But he swears to nothing. This covenant is mutual in the sense that there are two distinct parties who have a certain freedom and initiative in concluding it, but it is not mutual in the sense that an explicit *quid pro quo* is involved.

There is nothing in Exodus 20 like the list of divine witnesses which is so prominent a part of the treaties, and indeed it is difficult to see how this could have survived the transfer of the treaty pattern to the religious sphere. Even if we accept, as a hypothesis, that the Sinai covenant was a creative adaptation of a common legal form, calling on the gods hardly lent itself to use within Israel. A later paragraph will show how Joshua dealt with the idea of witnesses to the covenant: the people themselves are witnesses against themselves, or the stone he sets up is a witness, but the impression one has is of a somewhat awkward attempt to incorporate a traditional practice, and the very fact that the witness idea is dealt with twice in Joshua 24 seems to show that this feature cannot easily be fitted into a treaty with the God of Israel.[4] To jump ahead of the story again,

4. The matter of witnesses to treaties is complicated now by the publication of new treaties between the Hittites and tribes called the Kashkaeans on the border of the Hittite empire. Some of these treaties give the names of individual human beings who are witnesses to the pact, in some sense, if only to the formal preparation of the text. Divine witnesses are also included, however. Further study of these texts might eventually suggest modifications in our understanding of Joshua 24 and other biblical passages. For these treaties see Einar von Schuler, *Die Kaškäer* (Berlin, 1965).

we shall see in a later chapter that the prophets do preserve the idea of witnesses to the covenant, but it is very carefully employed to leave no doubt about Israelite monotheism and is at the level of metaphor.

The blessing and curse commonly found in treaties is reflected in Exodus 20, though it is not nearly as explicit here as it is elsewhere in the Bible. The word "curse" does not occur in the chapter, but the substance is there in the description of Yahweh as the jealous God who punishes sons for the fathers' iniquity. Breach of this covenant involves divine punishment against the offender and his whole household, down to grandsons and great-grandsons—a provision that recalls the treaty. Obedience brings blessings forever. The words "hate" and "love," used here of the two possible attitudes toward Yahweh, are also significant in this connection, though once again fuller proof will have to be brought in a later chapter. These terms, however obviously they point to the vocabulary of human emotions as their ultimate source, are best understood as reflecting the language and categories of international relations, where the saying was: "With my friend you shall be friend, and with my enemy you shall be an enemy." [5]

Exodus 20 then has only a brief counterpart to the blessings and curses of the treaty, and as will be shown below, in Exodus 24, which continues the Sinai story, the curse involved in the covenant with Yahweh is at best implied in the ritual sprinkling with the blood of the covenant. These two parts of the Sinai account, however, do not give a true picture of the extent to which the Old Testament connects covenant with curses and blessings. Elswhere in the Bible there are curses by the handfuls, especially in Leviticus

5. This is column ii, 3–4, of the treaty between Suppiluliumas and Tette, number 3 in E. F. Weidner, *Politische Dokumente aus Kleinasien*, Boghazköi Studien, no. 8 (Leipzig, 1923).

26 and Deuteronomy 28, which also contain briefer and more perfunctory blessings. It is fair to cite these lists here because both function in the same way as do the blessings and curses in the treaties, to encourage obedience to a code of behavior which has just been set forth. This is especially true in the case of Deuteronomy; the whole book is a covenant on a grand scale, with historical introduction, stipulations, and the closing blessings and curses in chapter 28. For the full effect of the chapter, the reader is urged to read the entire sixty-eight verses; only a few are rendered here, to give at least some impression of how liberally the Israelites employed this treaty feature in their religious thought. "Then if you really hearken to the voice of Yahweh your God, and are careful to do all his commandments . . . then all these blessings will come upon you and overtake you. . . . You will be blessed in the city, and blessed in the country. Blessed will be the fruit of your womb, and the fruit of your land. . . . Yahweh will put your enemies, those who rise up against you, to flight before you. By one way they will come out against you, and by seven ways they will flee before you. . . ." Such benedictions fill the first fourteen verses; the curses occupy the other fifty-four verses, or, to give another estimate, can be intoned aloud in about twelve minutes' time, an achievement in nonstop malediction which would have excited the admiration of Mark Twain. "But if you do not hearken to the voice of Yahweh, your God, and are not careful to do all his commandments and ordinances which I command you this day, then all these curses shall come upon you and overtake you. You will be cursed in the city, and cursed in the country. . . . cursed when you come in, and cursed when you go out. . . . And your sky o'er your head shall be copper, and the ground beneath you, iron." At points the curses are metrical, and form a grim ditty:

The maid that you wed
You will ne'er take to bed.
You will build a fine home,
But in exile you'll roam.
You will plant a vine,
But not drink the wine. . . .

Near the end stands a psychologically telling threat: "Your life will hang suspended before you, and you will be in terror night and day, and have no confidence in your life. In the morning you will say, How I wish it were evening! And in the evening you will say, How I wish it were morning!" And after one final curse, comes the conclusion: "These are the words of the covenant which Yahweh commanded Moses to make with the Israelites."

Returning to the Sinai narrative in Exodus, where is the oath? The oath is half the treaty. It is the feature that makes the terms binding on the vassal, and if it were not present in the Israelite covenant with God, then they would have departed very far from the form of treaty which was presented in the previous chapter. We would have only the voice of God and no "Amen" from the people. Exodus 20 itself contains no oath on the part of the Israelites, for after the announcement of the Ten Commandments comes only a description of the fear that fell upon the hearers and their desire that Moses should speak to them, not God. To discover the act of swearing by which Israel entered the covenant, we must look beyond Exodus 20 and skip over the long collection of laws which has been inserted between the Commandments and the continuation of the narrative in Exodus 24. Here we discover the sequel to the theophany at Sinai, or rather a double sequel, for intertwined within the compass of the first fourteen verses of Exodus 24 are two separate accounts. Chapter 24:1–2, telling how Moses, Aaron, Nadab, Abihu, and seventy elders are ordered to ascend the mountain, is interrupted by a separate story (3–8), only to pick up again in verses 9–11. When the results of a critical analysis are stated thus baldly they are apt to arouse the suspicion that some black art is being practiced, or that the critics are just guessing, but in effect this division into separate strands means that unless we divide the chapter in some such fashion it seems to be an unintelligible jumble. We will look first at the account in Exodus 24:3–8:

> Then Moses came and told the people all the words of Yahweh, and all the ordinances. And the people answered, with one voice, and said, "We will do everything that Yahweh has said." Then Moses wrote down all the words of Yahweh and rose early in the morning and erected an altar at the foot of the mountain, and twelve upright stones for the twelve tribes of Israel. And he sent young men of the Israelites and they offered up whole burnt-offerings, and sacrificed peace-offerings to Yahweh, bullocks. Then Moses took half of the blood, and put it in basins, and he sprinkled the other half of the blood on the altar. Then he took the text of the covenant and read it so the people could hear it, and they said, "All that Yahweh has spoken, we will do and obey." Then Moses took the blood and sprinkled it on the people and said, "Here is the blood of the covenant which God has made [literally, "cut"] with you, on these terms" (24:3–8).

This may well be the proper continuation of chapter 20.[6] Even if it is not, but is an originally separate tradition, it does show that one account connected the Sinai covenant with an oath by the people, for that is the significance of

6. Although it does not seem necessary for our purposes to go any further into the sequence of events in the "JE" account of Sinai, the reader may be interested in the plausible reconstruction carried out by Otto Eissfeldt. Eissfeldt would put most of Exodus 20:18–21 at the head of the chapter, before the commandments, giving this original sequence: the theophany (chapter 19), the fright of the people and Moses' ascent of the mountain (20:18–21), the decalogue given by God (20:1–17), the return of Moses and the oath (24:3–8). For further details and for Eissfeldt's account of how the material came to stand in its present disorder, see his *The Old Testament: An Introduction*, trans. Peter R. Ackroyd (New York and Evanston, 1965), pp. 212–13, 216–18.

Moses' actions. He tells them what Yahweh has said and thus offers them the covenant. They agree, informally. Thus the stage is set for the formal oath. Moses writes out a copy of the text. Animals are slaughtered, and half the blood preserved. He reads the final and binding assent. Then he sprinkles the blood on them and identifies it as "the blood of the covenant." The idea is similar to that involved in passing between the parts of an animal; the sprinkling with blood in a similar way establishes contact and identification with the victim. The thought is "May the Lord do so to me, and more also, if I go back on my word. . . ."

It is possible that the other little story in this chapter is also intended to relate the formal ratification of the covenant. It is quite different and almost shocking in the way it makes Israel's God very close to Moses and the elders. "Then Moses and Aaron, Nadab and Abihu, and seventy of the elders of Israel, went up and saw the God of Israel. Beneath his feet was something like a paving of sapphire, clear as the sky itself. And he did not raise his hand against the leaders of Israel. They looked at God, and ate and drank (Exodus, 24:9–11). Both among the modern bedouin and in the ancient Near East, one manner of making a league is for the prospective partners to eat together cere-monially, and perhaps that is what the author of these artless lines meant to say. This, then, would be his version of how the covenant at Sinai was ratified. But although this is possible, it remains less explicit than the other account in the same chapter.

Although Exodus does not contain any reference to pre-serving the text of the covenant, all are familiar with the "Ark of the Covenant," the box in which the two tables were laid and which stood in the Most Holy place. There was also a tradition within Israel of public reading of the covenant provisions.

Then Moses wrote down this law and gave it to the priests, the sons of Levi, who carried the ark of the covenant of Yahweh, and to all the elders of Israel. Moses commanded them: After seven years, at the appointed time for the year of release, at the feast of Booths, when all Israel comes to see the face of Yahweh your God, in the place which He shall choose, you are to read this law aloud so that all Israel can hear. Gather together the people, men, women, children, and the alien within your gates, that they may hear and learn and fear Yahweh your God, and be careful to do all the things in this law. And your sons who do not know it shall hear and learn to fear Yahweh your God, all the days that you live in the land which you are going to make your own after you cross the Jordan (Deuteronomy 31:9–13).

The style of the passage quoted marks it as relatively late; this is the elaborate rhetoric of Deuteronomy. But the practice itself seems to be old, for it was probably associated from early times with the ancient custom of the three pilgrimage feasts: Unleavened Bread, Pentecost (Weeks), and Booths. "Three times in every year every male of your number shall see the face of the Lord, Yahweh, the God of Israel," is commanded already in a very ancient passage, Exodus 34:24.

The name Shechem is not nearly as well known as Sinai, but the site is unusually impressive and the covenant concluded there is almost as important as Sinai's in the history of Israel. Shechem crouches in the pass between two imposing peaks, Ebal and Gerizim, and confronts a fair and fertile plain. It is to this strongly fortified city, sacred since the times of the patriarch Abraham, that Joshua gathers "all the tribes of Israel" and brings them into a covenant with Yahweh. This, of course, raises some questions, the main one being: Why this new covenant? Out of scraps of evidence in Genesis and Judges, and from the potsherds and walls and soil-layers turned up in a long series of excavations at the site, scholars have pieced together a plausible explanation of the solemnities described in Joshua 24. Shechem had been associated with the making of pacts long before the Israelites ever appeared on the scene. The very name of the founder of the town points to an association with treaty ceremonies, and the name of the god worshipped in its temple—the largest temple yet discovered in Palestine —is variously given as "God of the Covenant" (El Berit) or "Lord of the Covenant" (Baal Berit). The book of Joshua, which tells of how the Israelites conquered the promised land, omits any reference to a conquest of the territory later held by the tribes Ephraim and Manasseh, where Shechem lay, and there are other hints in the biblical record that Israel's origins and early history were not so unified as a casual reading would suggest. There were groups within later Israel which had not taken part in the exodus and had not stood at Sinai, and the classic league of twelve tribes comes into full existence only on the soil of Palestine —at Shechem, to be exact. Here we have an account of the definitive formation of the twelve-tribe league, incorporating peoples who may well have had ancient ties with Israelite tribes but who only now pledge their undivided allegiance to the God of Israel. So decisive is this act that Shechem becomes the center of the sacred league, and here, so the theory continues, was kept alive a tradition of periodic renewal of the covenant.[7] With this introduction, we now turn to Joshua 24 to confirm and fill out the picture of the covenant sketched on the basis of Exodus 20.

> Then Joshua gathered all the tribes of Israel to Shechem. He summoned the elders of Israel, and its chiefs, its judges and officers, and they took their stand before God. Then Joshua said to all the people: "Thus says Yahweh, the God of Israel: 'Your fathers dwelt in the land beyond the Eu-

7. For a more detailed presentation of the background of Joshua 24, see the chapter, "The Sacred Area of Shechem in Early Biblical Tradition," in G. Ernest Wright, Shechem: The Biography of a Biblical City (New York and Toronto, 1965), pp. 123–38.

phrates in olden times, Terah, the father of Abraham and Nahor, and they served other gods. Then I took your father Abraham from beyond the River and made him go through the whole land of Canaan. And I gave him increase of offspring, and gave him Isaac. Then I gave to Isaac Jacob and Esau. I gave Esau the mountain land of Seir for his own, but Jacob and his sons went down to Egypt. Then I sent Moses and Aaron and smote Egypt, with what I did in their midst, and afterward I brought you out. Then I brought your fathers out of Egypt and you came to the sea. The Egyptians were chasing after your fathers with chariots and horsemen, to the Sea of Reeds, so they cried to Yahweh and he put darkness between you and the Egyptians. Then he brought the sea over them and covered them up. Your own eyes saw what I did to Egypt. You dwelt in the wilderness many days. Then I brought you into the land of the Amorites, who dwelt on the other side of the Jordan, and they fought with you, and I delivered them into your hands, and you took over their land and I wiped them out before you. Then there arose Balak son of Zippor, king of Moab, and he fought with Israel. He sent and called Balaam son of Beor to curse you. But I was not willing to listen to Balaam, and he blessed you instead. Thus I delivered you from him. Then you crossed the Jordan and came to Jericho, and the lords of Jericho fought with you—the Amorites and Perizzites, and the Canaanites, and Hittites, and the Girgashites, the Hivites, and the Jebusites, but I delivered them into your hands. And I sent before you the *hornet* [traditional translation; meaning uncertain] and it drove them out from before you, that is, the two kings of the Amorites, without your sword and bow. I gave you a land for which you did not toil, you live in cities which you did not build, you eat of vineyards and olive groves which you did not plant.' Now then fear Yahweh and serve him in integrity and good faith. Put away the gods your fathers served in the land beyond the Euphrates, and in Egypt, and serve Yahweh. But if you dislike the idea of serving Yahweh, why, choose today whom you do want to serve, whether the gods your fathers served in the land beyond the Euphrates, or the gods of the Amorites in whose land you live now. But as for me and my family, we will serve Yahweh."

Then the people replied, "Far be it from us to forsake Yahweh, and serve other gods! For Yahweh is our God. He is the one who brought us and our fathers up from the land of Egypt, from the house of bondage, who did before our eyes these great wonders and guarded us on the whole way by which we came, among all the peoples through whose midst we passed. Yahweh drove out all the nations from before us, and the Amorites who dwelt in the land. We too want to serve Yahweh for he is our God." Then Joshua said, "You cannot serve Yahweh, for he is a holy God, he is a jealous God, he will not tolerate your rebellions and transgressions. When you forsake Yahweh and serve strange gods, he will turn around and do you evil and consume you as he once did you good." But the people said to Joshua, "No! For Yahweh is the one whom we will serve." Then Joshua said to the people: "You are witnesses against yourselves, that you have chosen Yahweh for yourselves, as the one to serve?" They said, "We are." "Then put away the strange gods which are among you and turn your hearts to Yahweh, the God of Israel." The people said to Joshua: "Yahweh our God will we serve, and to his voice will we hearken."

So Joshua made a covenant for the people on that day, and established an ordinance and customary observance at Shechem. Joshua wrote down these words to be a book of instruction from God,[8] and took a great stone and set it up there beneath the oak which is in the sanctuary of Yahweh. Then Joshua said to all the people: "This stone shall be a witness among us, for it has heard all the words of Yahweh, which he spoke to us, and it shall be a witness against you, lest you play false with God." Then Joshua dismissed the people, sending each one to his own inheritance.

Bearing in mind that we are dealing with a description of how a covenant was made, and not with the actual text of the covenant, we can detect in this chapter the same pattern of thought discovered in Exodus 20 and in the extrabiblical vassal treaties. The scene is Shechem, before the sanctuary. Joshua begins by identifying what he says as the words of Yahweh and then launches into a lengthy historical introduction presented as the direct speech of God, in the first person. The important thing is that the history is pre-

8. The conventional translation of these words is "in the book of the law of God" (so the Revised Standard Version). The rather interpretive rendering adopted here is intended to avoid some misconceptions that might arise from the literal rendering.

sented here not just as a tale of "old, unhappy, far-off things" but as the hearers' own experience, though it covers many generations, and as a record that puts them under an obligation. It is this similarity in function which justifies our calling this a parallel to the way history serves in the vassal treaty, in spite of the contrasts in detail to what was said in Exodus 20. Here we have a different beginning, for the narrative starts with the patriarch Abraham,[9] and it extends further, for it comes down to the conquest. But the stress is the same: the divine suzerain's gracious acts to his vassals culminate in a call for them to choose, with the proper choice clearly suggested. What else could they do but serve Yahweh, after all he had done?

We do not have any record of detailed stipulations—remember that this is not the covenant text itself. In offering the covenant, Joshua stresses only one thing: service of Yahweh to the exclusion of all other gods, in other words, the First Commandment. The "ordinance and customary observance" he established by covenant would no doubt have gone into more detail about what it meant to have only this one Lord, but the essential obligation of the covenant is stated plainly enough in the text as it stands. In somewhat the same way, there is an implicit blessing and curse, though nothing explicit. Before he permits the people to

9. Any explanation of the fact that Exodus 20 does not include reference to the patriarchs is inevitably speculative, but the following is at least possible. There is evidence for the view that traditions about Abraham, Isaac, and Jacob were preserved and handed down at various local shrines within Palestine. These traditions were known and cherished by various groups, including some who did not take part in the sojourn in Egypt, the exodus, or Sinai, and were not originally joined together into a unified account of Israel's origins. On this view, the brief history in Exodus 20, beginning only with the exodus, would preserve a very ancient tradition, and Joshua 24 would show the later state of affairs, when the patriarchal stories had been welded into a whole and introduced into the sacred covenant history.

involve themselves lightly in this most serious of relations, Joshua warns them of the possible evil consequences: God is "a jealous God," and to judge from their previous record, they are apt to fall into idolatry and incur his wrath. To put it in the terms we have been using all along, they would be bringing themselves under a curse, and their little exchange with Joshua on this score would be unintelligible without such an assumption.

"As for me and my family [house], we will serve Yahweh" establishes that entrance into this covenant with Yahweh was a matter for each individual family to decide, and much other biblical evidence points to the same conclusion. God's covenant was, of course, not with the head of the Israelite state, nor was it possible as far as we can tell for one tribal leader to commit a whole tribe. The sacred pact was concluded with individual families, and it remained the responsibility of each father to acquaint his children with its provisions. This is different from the situation in most Hittite treaties, which involve heads of state. The Israelite covenant in this respect is more like a small group of treaties between the Hittite king and the Kashkaeans, tribes who did not have a king. In these treaties individual Kashkaeans, presumably tribal leaders, are listed by name as partners.[10]

The idea of witnesses to the covenant at Shechem is dealt with in an inventive but rather clumsy way, as mentioned above. At one point the people are said to be witnesses against themselves, and then when the covenant is actually made, it is a stone which "has heard all these words" and which will witness against them. This is about as close as one could tread, within Israelite monotheism, to the notion of a divine witness, for a standing stone like this bore the name Beth-el, "House of God," among the Israelites and their neighbors. Even though within Israel there is no ques-

10. See n. 4 above for literature on the treaties with Kashkaeans.

tion of stones being regarded as deities separate from Yahweh, yet this great stone was in their view more numinous, more charged with supernatural power than it would be to us. A sacred stone—sacred to Yahweh, to be sure—is a reasonable approximation to a divine witness. Yet when all is said and done, a covenant with the one God as a partner practically precludes any real functioning of this part of the covenant form.

Joshua 24 offers an explicit parallel to normal treaty provisions for deposit in the sanctuary. Joshua wrote the covenant down, and evidently this "book of instruction from God" was to be kept at the sanctuary in Shechem. As mentioned above, many scholars believe that repeated reading of the covenant formed part of the year's religious ceremonies at Shechem.

To sum up, we seem to have an answer to the basic question raised in the first chapter: Israel took a suzerainty treaty as a model for God's treaty with her. Subsequent chapters will offer still more evidence on this score, but the picture is already clear enough for us to ask "Why?" Given the international situation and the political aims of ancient kings, it is fairly easy to figure out why the treaty assumed the shape it had in the second millennium B.C. But what was there about this sort of treaty which made it appeal to the Israelites as a way of expressing important convictions about God, about the relation between man and God, and between man and man? Of course we must not imagine the elders of Israel sitting in convention like so many founding fathers debating on a constitution for the new state, or like prelates in council arguing over the formulation of articles of faith. Even though the moment of emergence of the covenant idea is hidden from us, we may be sure that it grew out of experience, not out of abstract thought, and if we attempt to state express reasons for its adoption, we are only making explicit what must have been implicit and intuitive. To try to reduce the living reality of the covenant with God to a set of propositions is unsatisfactory in the same way that a verbal description of a symphony is. Yet the following may serve the function of program notes, to help identify the themes that make their appearance.

First of all, God is left free and sovereign. This sort of treaty puts a great king in league with others without reducing him to the status of an equal, and this expressed the way Israel thought of Yahweh. Since he does not swear to anything, there will not in the future arise any lawsuits against God. His own covenant cannot be used against him. At the same time, he is not thereby depicted as capricious. The covenant history shows his faithfulness and grace.

Israel too finds its proper place. There is respect for human freedom before God since entry into the covenant is initially a matter of choice. "If you dislike the idea of serving Yahweh, why, choose today whom you do want to serve. . . . But as for me and my family, we will serve Yahweh." Our thought about polytheism probably does not rise much above the level of Clough's "Thou shalt have one God only, who would be at the expense of two?" But the families who made up Israel knew very well the values represented by the gods whom their fathers had served and whom their neighbors served, and the choice was to them real and important. Though covenant meant that Yahweh had taken the initiative, he had not forced himself on an unwilling partner. Freedom is present in another sense also, for though some obviously unsocial acts are prohibited, Israel is left to develop according to what seems right in her own eyes. Finally, the covenant framework served to set in its place a potentially dangerous notion, the idea of election, the affirmation that Israel was the chosen people. Covenant contains this idea too, but combines it inseparably with the idea of obligation. Though a man's obligation toward others in his community is seen as an obligation to God, society, the state, is not deified. In the introductory chapter we speculated that covenant was apt to prove a rather complex idea, and at this point we can see that this was its virtue for Israel's religion. It combined in one scheme many of her most important beliefs and held them in a nicely adjusted balance.

We may go on to observe that the covenant idea played a large part in giving Israel's religion its distinctive character in comparison to the religions of her neighbors, almost as much as did her characteristic monotheism. Many of Israel's articles of faith, many of her religious terms, many of her ritual practices have counterparts in Babylon or Canaan. For example, the belief that God is a father, which offhand we might suppose to be particularly biblical, is completely undistinctive, as contemporary personal names show. Many ancient Semitic personal names are little sentences that assert something about a deity, and one of the commonest types is Abi-Baʿal, Abi-Dagan, Abiyahu, and so on, that is, "My father is Baal," or "Dagon," or "Yahweh," or almost any other god. In the same way many another detail of Israel's religion is nondistinctive; and the uniqueness of her faith lies in great part in its structure, in the interrelation of the parts, and here is where the treaty or covenant idea made an important contribution.

When are we to date the emergence of this covenant based on a suzerainty treaty? The dates of the documents available for study do not help very much. Our best sources for the covenant idea all date from centuries after Moses, and we cannot flatly assume that any of them give a true picture of what was already to their writers a rather distant past. On the other hand, we cannot make the equally naïve assumption that a late document contains no genuine information about earlier times. And since Israel's neighbors took relatively little notice of her, we have no body of direct external evidence for the sequence of events in her religious history. It would seem to be a game in which we have a large number of colorful and odd-shaped pieces and are at liberty to arrange them in a pattern that pleases us, but without much hope of being right. Yet there are some oblique approaches through which we may "by indirection find direction out."

We may begin by clearing the ground of one persistent fallacy, namely the idea that Israel's early faith was necessarily simple. Wellhausen objected to the covenant as a feature of Israel's early religion in part because he viewed early Israel as a primitive people, with a simple, natural, and direct relation to God, and there is something very satisfying to one's sense of order in the idea of progression from the simple to the complex, from the unreflective faith of a nomad people to the elaborate legalized covenant theology of a later day. The problem is that it is difficult to find any parallel for such a state of affairs in the ancient Near East in the late second millennium B.C. To medieval man, early Israel seemed to stand very close to the dawn of history, only a few generations from Adam, but now that we are acquainted in some detail with civilizations vastly older, we can hardly assume that Israel started from nothing in her religious evolution. Israel's neighbors were capable of creating elaborate mythologies and liturgies, of embodying theological reflection in cosmogonies, of hymning gods who were believed to rule the whole world, of framing poems on the subject of human suffering and divine justice—why should early Israel's creed have been nothing more than "Yahweh the God of Israel and Israel the people of Yahweh?" By this time the nature-gods of Mesopotamia had, as W. G. Lambert puts it, become civilized and were believed to be

organized into an order corresponding to the political structure of an earthly city. If so, why should the Israelites have
been incapable of drawing on a political analogy to express
religious ideas? None of this, of course, proves that early
Israel's religion took the form of a covenant with Yahweh,
but it at least shows that there is nothing inherently improb-
able in the view that so complex an idea was around from
the very beginning.

One positive reason for early dating of the covenant
with Yahweh is that this makes it possible to explain how
the twelve tribes of Israel lived together before there was a
king in Israel. Even if these tribes were blood descendants
of one man—the implausible view suggested by a casual
reading of the Bible—it is still hard to believe that they
existed side-by-side for over a century without a formal
agreement binding them. Such a situation just did not exist
in the ancient world. When separate groups confronted one
another, the choice was either a treaty or a fight. There was
no question of simply living for years without defining
mutual rights. The story of the ruse of the Gibeonites is
very instructive in this connection (Joshua 9). The existence
of a covenant becomes an even more necessary assumption
when one takes into account the biblical evidence that not
all those in Israel were blood kin. Passages in Exodus and
Numbers mention the presence of "a mixed multitude" or
"a great mixture" in the number of those that fled from
Egypt. The Old Testament also admits that the Israelites
fell short of making a complete end of those quaintly
named peoples so often listed together: "the Amorites and
the Perizzites and the Canaanites and the Hittites and the
Girgashites, the Hivites and the Jebusites." Thus although
we may accept as true that a sizable number of Israelites
escaped from Egypt and stood at Sinai (though not so many
as a later census list gives!), we must do justice to all the

evidence and say that early and late there were substantial foreign elements in Israel. If these diverse groups were nevertheless brought together into a durable league, what held them together? The bond was certainly not "natural." There is no trace in our records of a pact with a common human leader; Israel was not in covenant with Moses or Joshua. Nor do we find a widespread pattern of pacts between the tribes and clans, of Judah with Benjamin, and so on. What we do find presupposed in all our sources is Judah and Benjamin and the rest first of all in league with Yahweh, and through this bound to one another. One could go on to inquire whether it is necessary to assume that the federation of the twelve tribes had already taken place in the wilderness, before the conquest, or was formally sealed only after they were settled in the land, but it seems sufficient for our purpose to assert that the covenant with Yahweh comes very early in Israel's history.

Another route leads us to the same conclusion. Once there was a king in Israel, there was no promising soil left for growth of the idea of a covenant of the people with Yahweh, family by family.

We may close with a bit of external evidence. This chapter has been a comparison of biblical covenant patterns with a certain group of Near Eastern suzerainty treaties. What has not yet been said is that the form of the treaty changed over the centuries. This is most noticeable with respect to the historical prologue, that important part of the second-millennium treaties intended to move the vassal to loyalty. We have a fair number of later treaties, from the ninth through the seventh centuries B.C., mostly between the Assyrians and their vassals but also between kings of Aramaean states. In these there is no historical prologue, and, less important but perhaps significant, the list of curses grows longer and longer. The relation between lord and vassal now seems to be much more that of an overwhelmingly greater power over against a helpless underling. If we find in the Bible a great prominence given to the historical basis for Israel's obligation, we must conclude that she came under the influence of the covenant form early. By the time of the eighth-century prophets there was a different spirit and a different procedure in international affairs, one which could not have furnished the model for the kind of covenant pattern we have traced in Exodus 20 and Joshua 24 and will see underlying much more of the Old Testament.

To summarize, at some early date, probably even before the conquest, Israel entered into a covenant with Yahweh modeled on a particular sort of international alliance, a suzerainty treaty. Such a qualified, dry statement is enough for our purpose, and from this point we may proceed in the following chapters to trace the subsequent history of the covenant idea within Israel. It is obvious that certain important parts of the story are being left out, parts that are treated more boldly in biblical tradition. The Old Testament indicates that behind the forging of the tribes into a people bound by covenant was the force of a great man, Moses, and of an overwhelming experience, the theophany at Sinai. Of this nothing will be said here, out of a timidity that is perhaps justified. When scholars try to explain what happened at Sinai, they often seem rather like Cecil B. DeMille; they call on volcanoes, earthquakes, and thunderstorms like so many wind-machines and smoke-belchers in an attempt to explain the mystery by some conjunction of natural phenomena, succeeding only in rendering the miracle truly unbelievable. The Lord is not in the wind. It is safest to steer clear of this pitfall and get on with the story. Yet it seems essential at this point to interrupt our pedestrian account and quote a part of the superb prose narrative in which Israel preserved the memory of how God spoke the covenant, with a view to invoking something of the aura of holiness and mystery surrounding it in the mind of the ancient Hebrews.

And it came to pass on the third day in the morning that there were thunders and lightnings, and a thick cloud upon the mount, and the voice of the trumpet exceeding loud, so that all the people that was in the camp trembled. And Moses brought forth the people out of the camp to meet with God, and they stood at the nether part of the mount. And Mount Sinai was altogether on a smoke, because the LORD descended upon it in fire, and the smoke thereof ascended as the smoke of a furnace, and the whole mount quaked greatly. And when the voice of the trumpet sounded long, Moses spake, and God answered him by a voice [Exodus 19:16–19; Authorized Version].

CHAPTER FOUR

THERE WAS NO KING IN ISRAEL

The Jews well know their pow'r:
   e'r Saul they chose
God was their King, and God they
   durst depose.

John Dryden, Absalom and Achitophel

The Israelites of later times were of two minds about the days of the judges. On the one hand, since they were careful to preserve tales about these ancient heroes, we may assume that they were thrilled, as we are, by the fresh wild energy and the barbaric strangeness of their deeds. A more settled age must have regarded the era of the judges in much the same way that Americans look back on the Wild West. Imagine it! A woman leads an army to victory—three hundred men put an invader to flight—one man pulls down a temple, singlehanded! As is typical of Wild West tales, there are some stretchers—a thousand men with the jawbone of an ass is a bit strong—but the exaggerations do not so much distort the truth as heighten it, for these were marvelous and wild and bloody days. Yet along with the note of admiration which is still detectable in Israel's tales of Jephthah and Samson and Gideon and the rest, there is also an occasional expression of undisguised repugnance. The Israelites also thought it well, in telling of the judges, to include the case of the Levite and his concubine, where the themes of sodomy, rape, murder, and vengeance culminate in the final negative verdict on the period: "In those days there was no king of Israel; every man did what was right in his own eyes." This negative judgment is correct, of course, at least in the political fact it asserts. There was no king in Israel. And one could add other negatives which followed in consequence: there was no court; there were no courtiers. There was no extensive trade with other lands, for this went with kingship. There were no standing army, no monumental architecture, no royal tax-collector and no royal taxes, no royal decrees and no royal judges—in short, none of the liveliness and discipline and complexity that monarchy would one day bring. That being so, it might seem pointless to search here for the expression of political ideas, unless anarchy can be called a political idea. But there is another side of the period, one which the average Israelite under the monarchy would no longer have understood or appreciated very well. At the very end of the days when the judges judged, in the old age of Samuel, the last judge, when the people were clamoring for a king, Yahweh says to Samuel: "Obey the voice of the people in all that they say to you, for it is not that they have rejected you, but that they have rejected me from being king over them" (I Samuel 8:7). Here, as the theocracy comes to an end, we find a clear statement of what it was supposed to be all along: if there was no king in Israel, it was because Yahweh was king. Since we would trace the history of the covenant idea, then, our first task will be to study it when it was not an idea but a political and social reality.

Theocracy is, of course, an extremely elastic term, so flexible as to be relatively meaningless unless accompanied by some account of what practical shape the divine rule takes. "God is king" might mean, in fact, a society rigidly controlled by a caste of priests; or the equation may be "God is king, and the king is god," as in Egypt; or divine rule may be reduced to a vague notion of "this nation, under God." The particular shape which the rule of Yahweh took was none of the above but was in part determined by the nature of the pact between Israel and God.

Of course, the previous history of the tribal elements that formed Israel, the international situation, the geography of the land, and numerous other factors—including doubtless some of which we are at present ignorant—also went into making Israel what she was in pre-monarchic days. The covenant with Yahweh does not explain everything about early Israel, just as the federal constitution does not explain everything about the early days of the American republic. But it does help us to understand some things.

We may start by noting that the covenant was central, physically central we might say, in the organization of Israel. The point at which the heavenly sphere touched the earthly was the ark of the covenant. We have a highly artificial picture of the organization of Israel in "P," the Priestly document of the Pentateuch. Israel is pictured as a disciplined army with an elaborate plan for camping, and at the center of the sacred camp is the tabernacle, within whose heart stands the ark holding the two tables of the pact. Everything else in Israel is arranged around it, in descending order of holiness. As I said, this is artificial and in part even fantastic and anachronistic. The order of battle for an army on the march in holy war has been extended by the priest's imagination to a vast nation on her way through the wilderness. In the same way, the imagination of a later writer has given us a glorified picture of the tabernacle, has enlarged and gilded what was originally a much simpler portable shrine. Yet, as Frank Cross has shown, the tradition of a portable shrine, with the ark as its most holy object, goes back to earliest times and even has a prototype in the mythology of the Canaanites.[1] This shrine of the covenant was the focus of Israel's religious life.

1. See Frank M. Cross, Jr., "The Priestly Tabernacle," *The Biblical Archaeologist Reader* (Garden City, N. Y., 1961), pp. 201–28; reprinted from *The Biblical Archaeologist*, 10 (1947): 45–68. The last-

It is important to note that the ark meant more than the presence of God as an object of prayer and devotion. It played its part in making known the will of God, the divine sovereign. If God is king, then the question is: how does he give his orders? One important way was through the ark. The picture given in Numbers 7:89 is often repeated: "When Moses went into the tent of meeting to speak with him, he would hear the voice speaking to him from over the cover which is on top of the ark of the pact, from between the two cherubim." This association of revelation with the ark continues through the period of wilderness wanderings and until the end of the time of the judges. In the latter period we find the young lad Samuel "sleeping in the temple of Yahweh, where the ark of God was. And Yahweh called to Samuel . . . ." The reader may very well find this bare description unsatisfactory. What does it mean to say that Samuel heard a voice speaking, or that "Yahweh called?" Could anyone hear it, any time, or if not, what determined who could and when, or how did others decide that Yahweh had spoken to someone who claimed to have heard him? We are trying to get an idea of how, practically speaking, an invisible deity reigned, and it is frustrating to say that sometimes Yahweh issued his orders to people who were near the ark; it leaves off at the very point where our questions about the psychology of the thing begin. Nevertheless, it seems best not to go further, because from this point on we find almost pure speculation. Perhaps the most important observation we can make is that this was quite unproblematic for the writers of our texts. If it is a problem for us, they have not left us the means to solve it. Note, however, that to say Israel communicated with God at the ark is not simply

named periodical is highly recommended to those interested in up-to-date, nontechnical articles on the Bible as illuminated by recent discoveries.

another way of saying that Israel was controlled by the priests who controlled the tabernacle. The tabernacle, as we shall see, had no monopoly on divine oracles, nor was there an infallible technique for eliciting speech from the deity. God might speak thus to Moses or Samuel, but his word was not under human control. In the days just before Samuel "the word of Yahweh was a rare thing," and later, when a desperate King Saul inquired of Yahweh, "Yahweh did not answer him, neither by dreams, nor by the sacred lots, nor through prophets" (I Samuel 28:6). Thus there was a reality, recognizable to the Israelites, behind the idea that God spoke from over the ark of the covenant. If the precise nature of the phenomenon eludes our analysis, the conviction it points to is in any case what concerns us: the divine sovereign was believed to be present, and present for communication, at the place where the tablets of the covenant with him were preserved.

The same shrine also functioned as a center where memory of the covenant was kept alive. This is completely unmysterious and more readily comprehensible to us. The rule, already cited above, was that every Israelite male must appear before Yahweh three times a year, at the three great festivals. Scholars have tried to fix on one of the occasions as the great covenant festival, but it is likely that at each of the three pilgrimage feasts there was a recitation of the history and terms of the pact. Joshua 8 tells of a reading of the Mosaic covenant in the days of Joshua, and we may study it as perhaps typical of the form such a liturgical repetition of the treaty might take. Note that this incident is set in Shechem between Mt. Ebal and Gerizim. As observed in an earlier chapter concerned with Joshua 24, the ark was perhaps first located at Shechem (later it was at Shiloh). We are probably right, then, in thinking that the following narrative of what happened in Joshua's days may be taken as typical of the kind of covenant repetition which was repeatedly held at this sacred site.

> He [Joshua] wrote there on the stones a copy of the law of Moses, which he wrote before the Israelites. And all Israel, its elders, and officers, and judges, were standing on either side of the ark opposite the Levitical priests, who carried the ark of the covenant of Yahweh—both native-born and resident aliens were there, half on the side toward Gerizim and half on the side toward Ebal, as Moses the servant of Yahweh had commanded at the start, so as to bless the people of Israel. And afterward he read all the words of the law, both the blessing and the curse, just as it was written in the copy of the law. There was not one word of all that Moses commanded which Joshua did not read before the whole assembly of Israel, including the women and children and the aliens who went along with them (Joshua 8:32–35).

Note, too, that whenever an Israelite brought the first-fruits of his land to the tabernacle, as an offering to Yahweh, he was to recite before the priest: "My father was an Aramaean about to perish, but he went down to Egypt . . . ." and the rest of the covenant history (see Deuteronomy 26:1–11).

Moving out from the focal point, the ark and its shrine, we may consider the community that grouped itself about this center, the twelve tribes of Israel. A bright Sunday-school child might be able to recite the names of the twelve tribes, but the average biblical scholar would probably find it more difficult because early lists of the tribes differ. What this means is that the total, twelve, which is characteristic of most of the lists, was more important than the individual parts that composed it. If Levi is not counted as a tribe, then Joseph can be divided into Ephraim and Manasseh to make up the difference. Aside from any mystical significance that the number twelve may have had, and aside also from the tradition that this was a good number for a league of tribes, there may have been a practical reason for adherence to the number twelve: this number made it possible for each tribe to bear the cost of maintaining the central shrine for one month. Thus the political form early Israel assumed as a result of her covenant with God may be called a league of tribes for the maintenance of a central sanctuary. Roughly similar institutions existed among the ancient Greeks; for example, separate city-states joined themselves by pact to support the shrine at Delphi. Such a league was called an amphictyony, from the verb meaning "to live in the neighborhood" of a shrine, and this term is now very widely used to describe Israel in the days of the judges.

How close was this federation? Except for allegiance to the common sanctuary, how much unification of action did it bring about, and how much machinery was there for regulating inter-tribal affairs? Scholars' estimates differ because the evidence is scanty. We do hear of "chiefs" of the tribes (the Hebrew is nasi᾿), and it is likely that from time to time, perhaps at the religious festivals, these chiefs and other tribal dignitaries met to discuss matters that involved more than one tribe. But it is probably wrong to think of this as having been very highly organized. The covenant with God united the tribes but did not lead to the erection of any elaborate political organization. Indeed, that would have been a violation of the spirit of the arrangement, for when Joshua deals with the assembly at Shechem, we see that he speaks "for me and my family" and addresses those present in the same spirit, as individuals and heads of families. The league with God is directly with the smallest social units, and Israel is not a pyramid joined to the deity only at the top. In the days of the judges, then, freedom of action, and responsibility before God, was in the hands of families, clans, and tribes.

We are led, then, to consider the status of the individual Israelite under the covenant, and the most important thing has already been said: there is a fundamental equality of status so far as Yahweh is concerned, or to put things right way round, an equality of responsibility. The leader, Moses or Joshua or whoever, has a vital function at the conclusion of the pact with God, but, this concluded, he does not continue to stand between the people and God as an indispensable mediator. This fundamental equality is also reflected in the economic status of the people. The typical Israelite lived in a village and worked his own few acres. He was not much better off than the poorest man in the village, and few had much more than he. At this point the biblical picture is supplemented by archaeological finds, which show that early Israelite houses are of basically similar size and construction. Land was held as a direct fief from Yahweh and was inalienable, that is, it was an act of impiety against Yahweh and one's ancestors to sell or trade one's inheritance. That is what made Naboth so stubborn when, later on, King Ahab offered him a fair deal for his vineyard (I Kings 21). It might appear that this is natural, or obvious, or just what one would expect from people of a simple nomadic and pastoral background and that it has nothing much to do with the covenant with Yahweh. But such an objection would overlook the social system that Israelite egalitarianism replaced.

Syria and Palestine in the Late Bronze Age (the period at whose close Israel came into being) was a region of city-states; each separate section—and most of them were tiny—was under the control of a king. His fortress-city, with its towering thick walls and massive gates, looked down from a hill or rocky outcrop over the plains and hamlets which it dominated. The king was wealthy and so were his "servants," the chariot-warriors who held lands in fief from him. At the bottom, not quite slaves but not wholly free, was a wretched class of serfs. The serf's crops fed the wealthy, his lands might be granted to some royal favorite, his children would be taken as soldiers, and in the few times when he did not have to labor at his own lands he had to go build with his own hands the fortress city that oppressed him. Running through the Old Testament is a strain of delight at the fall of those on top in the social economic order and the rise of the lowly, notably in the early (perhaps tenth-century) song of Hannah:

> The bow of the warriors is broken,
> But the fallen gird on strength.
> The fat hire themselves out for bread,
> And the starving hunger no more.
> . . . .
>
> Yahweh makes poor and enriches,
> He humbles and he exalts.
> He raises the poor from the dust,
> Lifts the needy from the rubbish heap.
> Yea, he sets them with princes
> And grants them a glorious throne.
> (I Samuel 2:4–8)

In early Israel there is a deliberate rejection of the rigid order that oppressed the poor to maintain an elite, and this rejection we may assume is nourished on the one hand by the history of state-slavery in Egypt and wilderness wandering, and on the other by the history of oppression remembered by those Canaanite serfs who came to be numbered among the Israelites.

Democratization of religious responsibility meant that covenant traditions were kept alive in the individual family. This is a feature so characteristic of modern Jewish life, and of Christianity as well, that it takes an effort to recall that in the ancient East much of religion was a matter for the state: the gods were the gods of the city, and specialists, the priests, saw to the "care and feeding of the gods" and preserved the liturgy and mythology of the temple. If the common man was involved in all this, it was only through the temple, through his participation in what the officials in charge did there. From earliest times, of course, there were shrines in Israel with specialist priests and even a central shrine that had, as we have seen, special functions in preserving and transmitting the covenant. But along with this, the head of the individual family was charged with teaching his son of the sacred pact.

> In time to come, when your son asks you, "What is the meaning of the ordinances and the statutes, and the laws which our God commanded you?" you are to say to your son, "We were slaves to Pharaoh in the land of Egypt, and Yahweh brought us out of Egypt with a mighty hand and Yahweh performed great and calamitous signs and wonders on Egypt and on Pharaoh and on all his household, before our very eyes. But us he brought out of that place, in order to bring us in and give us the land which he promised by oath to our fathers. And Yahweh commanded us to do all these statutes, to fear Yahweh our God, for our continuing good, to keep us alive as it is today" (Deuteronomy 6:20–24).

"Every man did what was right in his own eyes" had as a corollary: "These words which I command you today, shall be before your eyes, and you shall teach them diligently to your sons" (Deuteronomy 6:6).

This decentralization had its advantages, but without some modification it would have left Israel at a disadvantage in two important activities: in war and in the exercise of justice. Both of these demand a concerted exercise of force, against the enemy in time of war, against the offender in the case of a crime that surpassed the ability of the smaller unit, the clan or tribe, to deal with it. Ultimately the tribal league failed over just these two problems, when pressures became extreme, but in the two centuries or so of its existence it did develop characteristic ways of dealing with war and wrongdoing, ways that reflect the underlying covenant idea. A central figure was the judge, who united in himself the tasks of war-leader and arbiter. The title "judge," though we retain it because it is traditional, is a bit misleading. We need to remember that in Israel, or among the Phoenicians or Carthaginians, where the title *shofet* (*suffete*) was also in use, the term was broader than our "judge." It is occasionally used as a synonym for "king" or "prince," to denote someone of highest authority who may exercise this authority in various ways, including that of deciding cases. It is still true among bedouin, for example, that people are ready to submit hard cases to a man with a reputation for prowess in war. He has the prestige to make decisions stick and has shown independence of mind and action. Similarly, in early Israel men who had made a name for themselves by exploits in battle might thereafter "judge Israel" for the rest of their lives. Our evidence leaves a great many questions unanswered about their role, but there is general agreement that they were what Max Weber called "charismatic" leaders.[2] There was no process by which one ran for judge, nor did one automatically succeed to his father's office as judge, though there were experiments along that line. Instead, it was a matter of a man's personal qualities: his strength, his decisiveness, his courage, his willingness to assume responsibility, and his luck. There is no need to go into detail here, for it is easy to find the proof of this by reading Judges. It is necessary, however, to see how the way the judges functioned reflects Israel's basic religious and social convictions: the man who is followed is the one in whom Yahweh's spirit has manifested itself.

Once Israel was in the Promised Land, war was called forth by some threat to her existence. There was no authority in firm enough control to rally the people for a war of foreign conquest. Since there was no standing army, when the Midianites or Philistines invaded it was up to some leader

2. Max Weber uses the term "charismatic" in many contexts in his classic contribution to the sociology of Israel which appeared in German in 1917–19 and is now conveniently available in English translation by Hans H. Gerth and Don Martindale under the title *Ancient Judaism* (New York, London, 1952).

to rally the tribal levy, sometimes of all Israel, often just of those tribes closest at hand. "The spirit of Yahweh clothed itself with" some Israelite, and he would blow a trumpet or send out messengers to gather others: "Follow after me!" A more impressive call was sometimes used. When the Levite's concubine had been abused and killed, he cut her up in twelve pieces and sent one to each tribe. Here we touch on the realm of the curse and thus of the covenant. A thing has been done in Israel of unheard-of wickedness, and the responsibility rests squarely on all, for the anger of Yahweh will fall on the whole people if they permit this kind of abomination in violation of their covenant. The Levite's gruesome act recalled and reinforced the curses attached to the covenant with God and summoned Israel to a battle that was Yahweh's. War belonged to Yahweh. Just as the great king, the Hittite king, obligated his vassals to fight for him, and just as this was the concern of the bulk of the treaty stipulations, so Israel had to fight for Yahweh, and the "wars of Yahweh" are the principal subject of the literature from this age. In one of our oldest pieces of Hebrew poetry, the Song of Deburah, there is a line that expresses perfectly the theory: "Curse Meroz! . . . Roundly curse those who dwell there! For they did not come to the help of Yahweh among the warriors" (Judges 5:23).

The idea that Yahweh was the divine suzerain, for whom Israel was to do battle as a loyal vassal, determined still more of the theory and practice of war. Recall that the vassal is sworn to fight "with all his heart" and is not to doubt and hang back because of the uncertainty of the outcome, as though to say, "I am under an oath of loyalty, but (how am I to know) whether they will beat the enemy or the enemy will beat them?" So in Israel the theory was that all Yahweh's battles are, in advance, victories. Israel is called on simply to trust this. Before the battle the word is:

"Yahweh has delivered them into our hands." There are many passages that reflect this theory, but two are especially characteristic and may be quoted almost without comment except to say that each in its own way is no doubt somewhat unrealistic, but for that very reason makes the theory stand out clearly.

> When you go forth to battle with your enemies, and see the horses and chariotry, and an army larger than yours, do not be afraid of them, because Yahweh your God, who brought you up from the land of Egypt, is with you. So when you draw near to the battle, the priest shall come forth and address the people, and say to them: "Hear, O Israel! Today you are going into battle against your enemies. Don't let your heart turn soft! Do not be afraid, and do not be shaken, and do not be terrified of them! For it is Yahweh your God who is going forth with you to fight for you with your enemies, to give you victory." Then the officers shall speak to the people; "Is there any man who has built a new house, and has not dedicated it? Let him go back home, lest he die in battle and another man dedicate it. Is there any man who has planted a vineyard, and has not yet enjoyed its fruits? Let him go on back home, lest he die in battle and another man enjoy its fruits. Is there any man who has arranged to marry a bride, and has not taken her? Let him go off home, lest he die in battle and another man take her." Then the officers shall go on and say to the people, "Is there any man who is afraid, whose heart is soft with fear? Let him go home, so that he does not make the heart of the others melt like his own" (Deuteronomy 20:1–9).

Note that these provisions are not just humanitarian but are intended to make as sure as possible that there will not be anyone in the ranks who does not have complete reliance on Yahweh. Parenthetically, it is interesting to note that the people of Ugarit also knew of the principle that the new bridegroom did not ordinarily have to go to war.

The second passage is too long for full quotation and perhaps too familiar to require it. This is the story of Gideon and the fight he led against the Midianites. The Midianites

were especially troublesome foes because they had camels. As
W. F. Albright has pointed out, the effective domestication
of the camel was rather recent, and so for the first time raiders
were able to go long distances through the desert without
water and to strike swiftly at the exposed flank of the Israelites. But "the Spirit of Yahweh clothed itself with Gideon,"
and the people consented to follow him. "Then Yahweh
said to Gideon, 'The force with you is too great for me to
deliver Midian into their hands. I do not want Israel to boast
at my expense and say, My own hand won me victory. Now
call out so the people can hear, Anyone who is afraid and
trembling, let him go back, and leave the hills of Gilead!' "
Twelve thousand go home, leaving ten thousand, whom
Gideon further reduces, at Yahweh's direction, to three hundred men. "That very night Yahweh said to him, 'Get up
and go down to the camp, for I have delivered it into your
hand.' " And victory follows, without a blow being struck.

The spoils belong to Yahweh, too. This is especially
clear from the story of Achan's theft (Joshua 7). Although
the spoils from Jericho were dedicated to Yahweh in advance,
Achan took for himself "one good Babylonian cloak, two
hundred shekels of silver, and a bar of gold weighing fifty
shekels" and concealed them beneath the floor of his tent.
In the next battle Israel was defeated and lost thirty-six men,
which terrified the people. "So Joshua tore his tunic and
lay down on his face on the ground until evening, both he
and the elders of Israel, before the ark of Yahweh, and they
put dust on their heads. And Joshua said, 'Ah my lord
Yahweh, why? . . .' Then Yahweh said, 'Get up. Why in
the world are you lying on your face? Israel has sinned.
Indeed, they have transgressed my covenant, which I imposed on them.' " So Joshua cast lots to determine the guilty
party. When it turned out to be Achan, he was urged to
confess, which he did. "Then Joshua took Achan son of

Zerah and the silver and the cloak and the bar of gold, and his sons, and his daughters, and his oxen and his donkeys, and his flocks and his tent and everything he had," and Joshua and all Israel "stoned him with stones, and burned them in fire, and stoned them with stones, so that they raised over him a great heap of stones."

Note the logic of the behavior here. Israel detects something amiss with God because a disaster has struck, and Joshua and the elders seek the reason at the most holy object, the ark of the covenant. They lie there until it is revealed to Joshua that the pact with God has been broken. Still uncertain as to the guilty party, Joshua casts lots—leaving it up to Yahweh to point out the one. The penalty is severe, but understandable. This is not the law of the Israelites in operation, for in an ordinary case at law only the guilty party suffered—certainly not his beasts—and he himself suffered only in proportion to the wrong he had done ("An eye for an eye and a tooth for a tooth"); Achan's wrong was in a totally different sphere. He had put Israel in the position of having broken the covenant with Yahweh; he had brought the curse of the covenant into operation, and this can be averted only by directing it onto the responsible party, with all he has, "his person, his wife, his son, his grandson, his house, his land and together with everything that he owns." I quote the curse commonly found in the Hittite treaties to show how thoroughly similar the line of thought is.

There are, of course, many features of Israelite warfare that do not flow directly from the idea of a covenant with God. It would be hard to show any direct connection, for example, between the sexual abstinence required of the warriors and the idea which is our theme. As Frank Cross and Patrick Miller, Jr., have shown in recent studies, some of the concepts and language used about Yahweh the Warrior derive ultimately from mythology.[3] The covenant does not explain *everything* about early Israel. Probably no society on earth is so tightly knit that everything in it is somehow functionally related to a central theme, and certainly early Israel was not. Even in those places where we can see the influence of the covenant idea, we can often see other ideas and institutions blended with it, as here. All that we may reasonably believe is that in the case of warfare we do not *fully* grasp Israel's practices unless we keep the covenant with God in mind.

If our hypothesis is correct, if the covenant with God was in a sense the constitution of early Israel, we would expect this to have affected the laws of the people also. We have already glanced at the role of the charismatic leaders, the "judges," in dealing with cases at law, but we cannot easily study their judicial careers, for the evidence is too meager. To study law and covenant we must look at the lists of laws that stud the book of Moses. The reader who tries to read the Bible like other books is apt to be confused or annoyed at the interruption of the story by bodies of laws—indeed it would be abnormal not to feel something approaching a personal dislike for the author of Leviticus. But if we feel that this is not a normal way to relate history, we may at least draw a profitable conclusion: this is in itself one of the marks that the covenant form has left on Israelite literature. Outside the Bible, it is in treaties that we find such a mixture of history and commands, and the present shape of the Pentateuch ultimately reflects the combination of narrative and obligation in the treaty. At the outset, then,

3. See Patrick D. Miller, Jr., "God the Warrior," *Interpretation*, 19 (1965): 39–46; and Frank M. Cross, Jr., "The Divine Warrior in Israel's Early Cult," in *Biblical Motifs: Origins and Transformations*, ed. Alexander Altmann (Cambridge, Mass., 1966), pp. 11–30.

we may feel assured that Israelite law is connected with the covenant idea. Yet we need to make a distinction. The Decalogue is not itself the law of the land. At least, it is helpful to separate it as something different from other formulations. George Mendenhall introduced to biblical studies a useful distinction between legal policy and legal techniques. The Ten Commandments are best understood as legal policy, that is, as a statement of those kinds of behavior which the community is willing to sustain by force. But there is no statement of just how an expression like "You shall not commit murder" is going to be enforced, or what steps Israel plans to take if the commandment is broken. Unless someone is willing to enforce it, such a statement is not a law. Contrast this with "If an ox gores a man or a woman, and the man or woman dies, the ox shall be stoned to death, and its flesh shall not be eaten, but the owner of the ox is free from blame." This states quite clearly the penalty the community will exact and the limit of the penalty. It is closer, then, to the realm of legal technique, to law proper. So it will be possible, and helpful, for us to compare the policy enunciated in the covenant stipulations and to see whether and how Israel reduced these to concrete laws. Note, however, that even the list of laws we shall study is not a code of written laws in the modern sense. If we were to think of, let us say, the Book of the Covenant (Exodus 20:22–23:33) as a law-code, we would immediately be struck by its inadequacy from the point of view of completeness and precision of formulation. In fact, there is no evidence that any collection of Near Eastern laws functioned as a written code that was applied by a strict method of exegesis to individual cases. As far as we can tell, these bodies of laws served educational purposes and gave expression to what was regarded as just in typical cases, but they left considerable latitude to local courts for determining the right in individual suits. They aided local courts without controlling them. Thus, in a sense, even a list like the Book of the Covenant belongs to the sphere of legal policy. Yet, if so, it still stands at a different level of concreteness than the Decalogue, and it will be instructive to compare these two.[4]

The Book of the Covenant is chosen for comparison because it is our earliest body of Israelite law. We cannot date it as early as Sinai because it is framed to fit a settled community living in villages and carrying on farming, not for dwellers in the wilderness. On the other hand, it is early as is shown by its language and by the fact that Deuteronomy (seventh century B.C.) presupposes it. Disregarding the question of whether there are some later accretions, there is general agreement that this slice of material comes from the first years of the monarchy or even earlier. Of course, this date is assigned only to the collection as a whole—individual laws, like the one quoted which concerns the goring ox, may have a prehistory that can be traced in Mesopotamian law a thousand years earlier.

> You shall not have other gods besides me. You shall not make yourself a graven image, or a likeness of anything in heaven above or in the earth beneath, or in the water under the earth. You shall not bow down to them or serve them.
> Exodus 22:19——A man who sacrifices to any god, except Yahweh alone, shall be put under the ban [that is, sentenced to death].

> Remember the Sabbath, so as to keep it holy. Six days you shall labor and do all your work, but the seventh day is a day of rest, belonging to Yahweh your God. You shall not do any work. . . .

4. Mendenhall's essay on Israelite law is the first half of his *Law and Covenant* (see Suggestions for Further Reading). Another important study which has been drawn on here is Albrecht Alt, "The Origins of Israelite Law," *Essays on Old Testament History and Religion*, trans. R. A. Wilson (Oxford, 1966), pp. 79–132.

Exodus 23:12——In six days you shall do your work and on the seventh day you shall rest, so that your ox and ass may rest, and so that your home-born slave may be refreshed, and also the alien.

Compare Exodus 31:14——You shall observe the sabbath, for it is a holy thing to you; he who profanes it shall be put to death.

Exodus 35:2——And on the seventh day you shall keep a sacred observance, a sabbath of rest belonging to Yahweh. Anyone who does work then shall be put to death.

Honor your father and your mother, so that your days may be long in the land Yahweh your God is going to give you.

Exodus 21:15, 17——He who strikes his father or mother shall surely be put to death.

He who reviles his father or mother shall surely be put to death.

You shall not commit murder.

Exodus 21:12–14——He who strikes a man a fatal blow shall surely be put to death. But he who did not act deliberately, it being an act of God—I will designate a place for you whither he may flee. But if a man maliciously plotted against his neighbor to slay him by a trick, you shall take him to be executed, even from my altar.

Exodus 21:18–25——If men are quarreling, and one man strikes the other with a stone or a hoe, not fatally, but so that he is confined to bed, if he gets up and can walk about outside with a cane, he who smote him shall be free of blame, only he shall pay for his support meanwhile and the medical costs. If a man strikes his slave, male or female, and it dies by his blow, he shall be liable to requital. But if he survives a day or two, he shall not be liable to requital, for the slave is his property.

If men are struggling, and they strike a pregnant woman, and she has a miscarriage, with no further injury to herself, a fine shall be imposed as the husband of the woman shall determine, the amount being fixed by estimate (of the age of the fetus).[5] If there is further misfortune, you shall require

5. The Hebrew is difficult here. The translation given is based on the study by Ephraim Speiser, "The Stem *PLL* in Hebrew," *Journal of Biblical Literature*, 82 (1963): 301–6. Note the parallel Speiser

a life for a life, eye for eye, tooth for tooth, hand for hand, foot for foot, burn for burn, wound for wound, bruise for bruise.

Exodus 21:28–32——If an ox gores a man or woman to death, the ox shall be stoned, and its flesh shall not be eaten, but the owner of the ox is free from blame. But if the ox had a fixed habit of goring, and sworn testimony to that effect was given to its owner and yet he did not watch it (or, perhaps, dehorn it), and it kills a man or woman, then the ox shall be stoned and also its owner shall be put to death. If a compensation in money is imposed on him, he shall pay the ransom for his life exactly as it is imposed on him. If it gores a minor, boy or girl, the same principle applies. If it gores a slave, male or female, he shall give thirty shekels of silver to the slave's owner, and the ox shall be stoned.

Exodus 22:1–2——If a thief is caught breaking in and is struck and dies, there is no blood-guilt for killing him. But if it happens in broad daylight, there is blood-guilt for him.

You shall not commit adultery.

Exodus 22:15–16——If a man seduces a virgin, who was not betrothed, and lies with her, he shall make her his wife by paying the bride-price. But if her father refuses to give her to him, he shall pay money equal to the bride-price for virgins.

Compare Deuteronomy 22:22–27——If a man is caught lying with a married woman, both of them shall die, the man who lay with the woman, and the woman. So you shall remove the evil from Israel. If it was a girl, a virgin, who was betrothed to a man, and a man comes upon her in the city and lies with her, you shall take both of them out to the city gate and stone them to death with stones—the girl because she did not cry out in the city, and the man because he violated the wife of another man. So you shall remove the evil from your midst. But if a man came on a betrothed girl in the country and seized her and lay with her, only the man who lay with her shall die. You shall do nothing to the girl. She has done no wrong deserving death, for this case is like that of a man who attacks another man and kills him, for he caught her in the country. The betrothed girl may have cried, but there was no one to rescue her.

---

cites from Hittite Laws I, 17: "If anyone causes a free woman to miscarry, then if [it is] the 10th month, he shall pay 10 shekels, if the 5th month, he shall pay 5 shekels."

You shall not steal.

Exodus 21:37–22:3——If a man steals an ox or a sheep and slaughters it or sells it, he shall restore five head for an ox, or four head for a sheep. . . . He shall make restitution. If he has nothing, he shall be sold for his theft. If what was stolen is found in his possession, alive, whether ox or donkey or sheep, he shall restore double.

Exodus 21:16——He who steals a man, whether he has sold him or is caught with the man in his possession, shall be put to death.

You shall not swear falsely by the name of Yahweh your God, for Yahweh will not acquit anyone who swears falsely by his Name.

You shall not give false testimony against your neighbor.

Exodus 23:1–2——You shall not spread a false report. You shall not make common cause with a man who is in the wrong, to give false testimony (for him). You shall not go along with the majority in doing wrong, or testify in a lawsuit so as to fall in with the majority and pervert justice.

Compare Deuteronomy 19:16–21——If an unscrupulous witness attacks a man by testifying that he committed a serious crime, the two men who figure in the suit shall stand before Yahweh, before the priests and the judges of that time, and the judges shall make a thorough inquiry. If the witness is a perjurer, one who gave false testimony against his brother, you shall do to him as he plotted to do to his brother, and remove the evil from among you. Those who are left will hear and be afraid; they will not do an evil thing like that at another time in your midst. And you shall not spare him— life for life, eye for eye, tooth for tooth, hand for hand, foot for foot.

You shall not covet another man's house. You shall not covet another man's wife, or his slave, male or female, or his ox or his donkey or anything that belongs to someone else.

(No corresponding law is recorded.)

The foregoing makes it clear that there is a rather close correspondence between the policy statements of the covenant and the concrete laws that instructed the judges of Israel. "So you shall remove the evil from your midst" is the recurring motive cited for the Deuteronomic laws, and this makes explicit the underlying assumption: that wrongdoing constitutes an offence to the divine overlord and is thus a threat to the group, an evil that must be rooted out. For nearly every statement of the Decalogue one can discover a corresponding law; in some cases there is no such law in the Book of the Covenant, but this is probably because it is incomplete. There seems to be little risk of distorting the picture if we fill in the holes from other lists of laws. We may doubt that the death penalty for Sabbath-breaking was very often carried out, but the extreme penalty was probably the one the theory called for, at any rate. It is of special interest to find that the First Commandment is also reinforced by the death penalty in this very early code. Scholars may argue about whether the faith of early Israel was monotheism, but chances are an early Israelite would have found the debate overly academic. All he knew was that if he offered a sheep to any god but Yahweh the law said he should die for it. The ancient story of what happened when the Israelites joined in worship of the Baal of Peor illustrates this point, as the story of Achan illustrates the theory of the holy war. According to Numbers 25, the Israelites in the wilderness began to intermarry with, or simply have intercourse with, the women of Moab and to join them in the feasts in honor of the local deity, the Baal of Peor. A plague broke out, which was understood at once as from the hand of Yahweh. The Israelite judges resolved that all those who had "yoked themselves" to the Baal of Peor must be killed. One priest, Phineas, took bold action and killed an Israelite and his Moabite partner *in flagrante delicto*. Then the plague stopped. The story rests on very ancient tradition and was firmly embedded in Israelite sacred history in a form that blamed Balaam for the whole affair. It shows that even if Israel was a long time in formulating an explicit abstract statement of monotheism, a practical, implicit monotheism that contrasted sharply with the tolerant polytheism of her neighbors was believed from very early times.

In many cases death is prescribed for transgression of any of the commandments, but this calls forth definition and qualification in law. This is especially true of the laws on homicide, where some basic distinctions are made between willfull and unpremeditated murder, accident with or without contributory negligence, and so on. Adultery is also defined; the Book of the Covenant states only half of it and needs the provisions of Deuteronomy for clarification. Adultery is a crime against the husband of a married woman, and thus the law divides cases according to whether the woman was married, which includes girls betrothed to a man by payment of the bride-price, or unmarried. If the girl is an unbetrothed virgin, this is not adultery but only an injury done to the girl's father, who might have trouble finding her a husband.[6] Theft, however, is not punishable by death, and restitution is regarded as sufficient to "remove the evil from your midst." This is the general principle in the realm of these laws: punishment or restitution in proportion, not exceeding the seriousness of the injury done. Remember that early Israel was made up of various groups and that in a truly primitive state of affairs a costly blood-feud is the answer to homicide or even to lesser offences. "Life for life, eye for eye" means that the community will not tolerate retaliation greater than the actual injury done.

But if we can see that Israelite law embodied the

6. For details on ancient Near Eastern legal precepts concerned with these matters and an example of the kind of comparative study of ancient laws that is now possible, see J. J. Finkelstein, "Sex Offenses in Sumerian Laws," *Journal of the American Oriental Society*, 86 (1966): 355–72.

principles of the covenant with Yahweh, it is plain at the same time that there is a genuine difference between the policy statements of the covenant and the law of the land. This is clearest with respect to the commandments about coveting. A greedy itch for the property and wives of others was clearly felt to be a serious threat to the internal peace of Israel, and thus "You shall not covet" is part of the covenant. But Israel's law, even if not a code in our sense, is a statement of what, practically speaking, the Israelites agree to do about violations of the "You shall not's"; and in the case of coveting, Israelite law says nothing at all. A man may be a mere whited sepulchre, but until the inner corruption becomes an action that someone can witness and testify about in court, the law has nothing to do with him. This means that whether we use Mendenhall's terms "policy" and "technique" or others, we will do well to make some distinction between these two levels at which the social values of Israel were expressed. This will be especially helpful when we attempt, later on, to deal with the views of St. Paul about the covenant, where Mt. Sinai is the symbol of law, and "gendereth unto bondage," like Hagar the bondwoman.

"There was no king in Israel; every man did what was right in his own eyes." These ambiguous words have a positive sense, if the picture drawn here is correct. The "King Immortal, Invisible," exercised a loose but effective rule through the central shrine and oracle, through inspired heroes and arbiters, through a recognized form for the conduct of war, and through the pressure of Yahweh's covenant terms on the shape of Israel's laws. At the same time, tribes, clans, families, and individuals enjoyed the maximum freedom of action. This lasted for perhaps two hundred years, and as forms of government go, cannot be considered an abject failure. Yet the Israelites themselves came to regard the theocracy as a failure, not without reason. Part of it was military. A well-trained, well-armed, and disciplined military force could beat Israel's irregulars nine times out of ten, unless "the stars in their courses" fought against them. The flourishing of the amphictyonic league coincided with the weakness of all the major powers around Israel— there was no threat from Egypt, Asia Minor, or Mesopotamia, but even so the Israelites had trouble beating back the little aggressors around them, especially the tough league of Philistine cities along the southern coast. If there was no king in Israel, "There was no smith in Israel" either (I Samuel 13:19). During this period of transition from use of bronze for weapons and tools to use of iron, the Israelites were dependent on the Philistines for any blacksmith work and were thus at a military disadvantage. When the Israelites brought the ark of the covenant into battle against their uncircumcised foes, the disaster was compounded: the ark was captured. Even though it was eventually returned, the Israelites quite naturally wanted a king who would "go out before us and fight our battles" (I Samuel 8:20).

Justice broke down, too, an especially dangerous case being that of the Levite and his concubine—"Nothing like this was done or seen from the time the Israelites came up out of Egypt unto the present" (Judges 19:30). A certain Levite, a man who lived in the territory of Ephraim, had taken a concubine of the town of Bethlehem. She ran away to her home, and he brought her back, the girl's father treating him with great cordiality. But he timed his trip north badly, so that nightfall overtook him near Gibeah, just north of Jerusalem, in the territory of Benjamin. A citizen of Gibeah received him kindly and took him and his woman in for the night. But as they were enjoying the evening meal, some riff-raff of the town surrounded the house, beat on the old man's door, and demanded, "Bring out the man who came into your house so that we may have intercourse with him." When the host refused, they clamored even more, until the Levite took his concubine and gave her to them. They abused her all night, until dawn, and left her dead. The Levite carried her body home, then cut it into twelve pieces and sent one to each tribe, calling on them to punish this abomination. The crime was senseless and brutal enough, but the worst aspect, for Israel as a whole, was what followed. Benjamin refused to give up those who were responsible, and the result was a conflict that almost destroyed Benjamin. "And they said, 'Why O Yahweh, God of Israel, did this happen in Israel, that today there should be lacking one tribe from Israel?' " The answer was evident. Peace, justice, and safety were dependent on the willing submission of the tribes to the covenant. Where this was lacking, where a tribe was willing to harbor rapists and murderers, the only recourse was to a bloodfeud which hurt the innocent along with guilty and threatened to destroy all Israel.

CHAPTER FIVE

NOAH, ABRAHAM, DAVID

In Milton's familiar line Saul is "He who seeking asses, found a kingdom." True enough, but what this poetic biography leaves out is that, having found the kingdom, he went home to his father's asses.[1] There was not much else for Israel's first king to do. Before Saul could play the role of king, he had first to write the part. There was no tradition in Israel of what a king was supposed to be or do, and at first things remained very much as they had been under the tribal league. In all likelihood, there was no universal agreement that Saul was a king (Hebrew *melek*) like other kings. Many people no doubt thought that he had been designated only as *nagid* (military commander), or perhaps *nasi'* (tribal chief). These titles of dignitaries under the tribal league survive here and there in our sources as titles for the early kings, and though *melek* now stands in most passages, it is probable that the less pretentious terms were more common in earlier forms of the stories than in the present form. The situation is much like that in the Roman Empire, where the title "king" was avoided, and republican titles like *princeps*, "chief citizen," and *imperator*, "commander," were used for the head of the state. The difference is that in the early days of Israelite kingship the substance of power was also lacking.

1. That is, if we take the story of Saul's rise as related in our Bibles. In actuality, two or perhaps three separate accounts of how Saul became king have been combined in I Samuel 8–13, so that it is difficult if not impossible to reconstruct the actual sequence of events. For more detailed information, see John Bright, A History of Israel (Philadelphia, 1959), pp. 166–68.

A wave of popular sentiment had called "Give us a king to rule over us," but there were also voices to say, "How shall this man bring us victory?" When Saul did bring victory, it was thoroughly in the fashion of the traditional charismatic leader. This enormously increased his prestige but was only a first step to establishing a monarchy "like all the nations." It remained to persuade the people to accept the idea of a dynasty, to establish a capital and an administration, to gather a standing army, and to work out a favorable relation with the national religion.

In this last respect Saul failed. Because the people had thought of themselves for centuries as a theocracy, it was absolutely necessary for the king to find some way of fitting himself into this religious picture. Remember that there was little or nothing that was secular in our sense, and no chance at all that an important institution like that of the kingship could remain outside the domain of the holy, that it could be separate from the religion of Yahweh. Saul had been anointed by Samuel, the chief representative of the old order. He made a further promising step when he gathered up the remains of the clergy who had served at the old shrine at Shiloh, now in ruins, and installed them in Nob, close to his rude fortress at Gibeah. But he was clumsy in his dealings with Samuel, the old priest and judge who would not easily give up his prestige as leader of the tribal league. In the end, half-maddened with suspicion of his young rival David, Saul completely alienated religious elements by ordering the slaughter of the priests at Nob.

By way of contrast, the young David reminds us of the angel in Blake's poem who "without one word spoke had a peach from the tree, and 'twixt earnest and joke enjoy'd the lady." Whatever he did turned out right, and convenient things, like the death of his enemies, happened without his having to do anything. Yet debunking does not really work on David. It can uncover no new faults, for such dark deeds as the murder of Uriah for the sake of Bathsheba are already stated quite plainly in the record, and it cannot diminish his real achievements. David made all the steps necessary to organize Israel into a kingdom. We are not concerned with sheerly political or administrative or military affairs (David succeeded there, too), but will consider briefly David's measures to tie himself and his dynasty to Israel's religion. A survivor of the old priesthood, Abiathar, became David's chaplain and, ultimately, high-priest. The prestige of another important group, the prophets, was tied to David in the persons of Nathan and Gad. Having selected and conquered an ideal new site for a capital, David built a palace there and wanted to put a temple, a royal chapel, next door. Though accomplishment of this was left to the reign of his son, Solomon, David himself danced before the ark, as his men brought it back from its wanderings, and installed it in a semi-permanent shrine at Jerusalem. The city of David would now become the pilgrimage center for all Israel. No blunders in all this, no slaughter of priests, no serious quarrel with the representatives of religion which could force anyone to choose between God and the king.

All these are practical steps. Along with them went the development of theories which explained how kingship fit with Yahwism. The grumbling "They have rejected me from ruling over them" would not do. Some positive account had to be given of how this new third element, kingship, fit into the old scheme of only two partners, Yahweh and Israel.

An important direction the theorizing took was the development of a different view of the covenant with God. It was not invented at this time. There were existing traditions of God's pact with the patriarchs on which David's priests and prophets and hymn-writers could draw. This does not mean that the biblical order, adopted here, necessarily reflects the chronological order in which these covenant traditions arose. The passages that treat the covenants with Noah and Abraham belong to the Priestly source and to "J," and thus in their present form are later than the introduction of the monarchy. But the archaic elements in the "J" account of Abraham's covenant do suggest that the traditions on which it rests are of very high antiquity, so that it seems permissible to take up Noah and Abraham before David, rather than the other way around.

> Then God said to Noah and to his sons along with him, "I am hereby establishing my covenant with you and with your descendants after you, and with every living thing as well including birds, cattle, and every wild beast, everything that came forth from the ark. . . . I establish my covenant with you, that never again will all flesh be wiped out by the waters of the deluge, and that there will not be another deluge to destroy the earth." So God said: "This is the sign of the covenant which I am making between me and you, and every living thing along with you, for all ages. I set my bow in the clouds, so that it may be a sign of the covenant between me and the earth. And when I gather clouds over the earth, the bow will appear in the clouds. Then I will remember my covenant, the one between me and you and every living thing, all flesh, and the water shall not again come as a deluge to destroy all flesh. The bow shall be in the clouds, and I shall see it and remember the everlasting covenant between God and every living thing, all flesh which is on earth." Then God said to Noah, "This is the sign of the covenant which I have established between me and all flesh on earth" (Genesis 9:8–17).

This is a covenant, unmistakably, because the same Hebrew word used for the Sinai pact, berit, occurs repeatedly here. It is also between God and man, involves an obligation that is binding "for all ages," and God takes the initiative. Beyond these generalities, there is not much resemblance to the Sinai covenant; on the contrary, it contrasts both formally and, more important, in intention. There is no history as a basis for the covenant. There is no obligation whatever laid on Noah and his descendants, expressed or implied. This is simply a unilateral promise of God, and it makes no difference what Noah does. Even human corruption will not change it; in the promise contained in the "J" account, the author repeats the very words that motivated the flood in the first place: God will not destroy the world by flood again, "for the thoughts of a man's mind are evil from little up." The same idea is implied in "P." Even if man is hopelessly corrupt, God will not again destroy him. The obligation is on God. It is he who in time to come will have to "remember" the covenant, and the "sign" of the covenant is for God to see so that he does not forget. We do not have here any explicit curse under which God brings himself, yet the writer of the medieval play *Noah's Flood* is essentially right in his quaint explanation of the meaning of the bow:

> My bow between you and me
> In the firmament shall be,
>
> . . .
>
> The string is turned toward you
> And toward me is bent the bow,
> That such weather shall never show,
> And this beheet I thee.[2]

God is bound here, and man is free.

The covenant with Abraham is similar in intent. Here we have two versions, again from "P" and "J," and we need to consider both. Genesis 15, the "J" account, tells how Abraham, lacking an heir, wanted to adopt Eliezer of Damascus. Yahweh rejected this and brought Abraham out to count the stars; so numerous should his descendants be. Abraham believed, and Yahweh "counted it to him for righteousness."

> Then he said to him, "I am Yahweh, who brought you out of Ur of the Chaldees, to give you this land as your own."

2. Quoted from A. C. Cowley, *Everyman and Medieval Miracle Plays* (London, 1956), p. 49, ll. 365–71.

He said, "Yahweh, my lord, how do I know that it will be mine?" Then he said to him, "Take a heifer three years old and a goat three years old and a three year old ram, and a dove and a young bird." So (Abraham) took all these things, and he cut them in two down the middle, and set the halves opposite each other. But he did not divide the birds. When carrion-birds came down on the dead bodies, Abraham chased them away. Just at sunset, a deep sleep came over Abraham, and terror, a great darkness, fell upon him. Then he said to Abraham, "Know this for sure, that your descendants will live as aliens in a land not theirs, and they will be enslaved and afflicted, four hundred years. But I will judge the nation whom they will serve, and afterward they will go forth with great possessions. And you shall go to your fathers in peace. You will be buried after reaching a good old age. And the fourth generation shall return to this place (for the iniquity of the Amorites is not yet complete)." When the sun sank, and there was dense darkness, a smoking brazier and a burning torch appeared passing between the cut-up pieces. On that day Yahweh made a covenant with Abraham: "To your seed I give this land, from the river of Egypt up to the great river, the Euphrates" (Genesis 15:7–18).

Like the covenant with Noah, that with Abraham binds only God. God obligates himself here to give Abraham Canaan, "the land of the Amorites." What makes this ancient account eerily impressive is the bold way in which it depicts Yahweh as swearing to Abraham. Abraham makes all the preparations for a covenant ceremony; he splits up animals and arranges the parts for the swearing of an oath. Then he falls asleep, and Yahweh, as a smoking oven and a flaming torch, passes between the parts. The author is discreet; he does not flatly say that Yahweh invokes a curse on himself. But the vision he has related makes the literal restatement unnecessary, and the imagination of the reader can supply: "Just as this heifer is cut up, so may I . . . ." This shares with Sinai only the name "covenant"; the roles of the partners are strikingly different.

The version given by "P" (Genesis 17) is translated here in abridged form. God speaks to Abraham:

"I establish my covenant between me and you, and your descendants after you throughout their generations, as an everlasting covenant, that I will be your God, and the God of your descendants after you. And I will give you and your descendants after you the land in which you have sojourned, the whole land of Canaan, as an everlasting possession, and I will be their God."

Then God said to Abraham: "And you shall keep my covenant, you and your descendants after you throughout their generations. This is my covenant . . . . Every male of your family shall be circumcised. You shall be circumcised in the flesh of your foreskins, and it shall be for a sign of the covenant between me and you . . . . It shall be my covenant in your flesh, as an ever-lasting covenant. Any male who is not circumcised in the flesh of his foreskin shall be cut off from his people; he has broken my covenant."

The substance is once again that God will give Abraham and his descendants "the land in which you have sojourned, the whole land of Canaan." The element that may be slightly confusing is the command that Abraham and his male offspring should be circumcised. This is "keeping" the covenant with God and might at first lead us to think that we have here an obligation comparable to the stipulations imposed by the covenant at Sinai. A closer reading of the chapter shows that this is not so; the "P" view of the agreement with Abraham is like that of "J" even if not expressed so drastically. Circumcision is "the sign of the covenant between us" (17:11). It is a mark to identify those who share in the promise God makes and functions like the rainbow to make God remember his own. Of course, anyone lacking this sign does not receive his share, but this is still not a command like those of the Decalogue. The setting and function are quite different. When St. Paul contrasts law and promise and declares: "God gave to Abraham through a promise," we have to admit that at this point he is right.

It would be going too far to say that this sort of covenant represents a religious idea contradictory to the Sinai covenant.

As we saw, a pact like that reported in Exodus 20 lays obligations only on the subjects, and yet the Lord, it is assumed, will also behave in a just and righteous way. It is not an instrument for establishing a tyranny. Conversely, even though a covenant like that with Abraham does not spell out how Abraham is to behave, it is assumed in the relation—that of having Yahweh as God—that Abraham will continue to trust God and walk righteously before him. Yet, granting all this, the emphasis in each of the two is so different that they come very close to being opposites.

To date no extra-biblical model for the type of pact represented by those with Noah and Abraham has been identified. Royal grants, as one might expect, were common in the ancient world, and numerous examples have survived of an outright gift by a king to a subject, whether of land, freedom from feudal dues, trading privileges, or whatever. A typical brief example runs as follows: "From this day forward Niqmaddu son of Ammistamru king of Ugarit has taken the house of Pabeya [. . .] which is in Ullami, and given it to Nuriyana and to his descendants forever. Let no one take it from the hand of Nuriyana or his descendants forever. Seal of the king." [3] The general resemblance to the one-sided grant to Abraham is obvious, but so is the contrast. Especially in the "J" account, it is clear that Yahweh takes an oath, and in other passages the promise of Canaan is frequently said to have been "sworn" by Yahweh. The royal grant quoted contains no oath; it is simply issued under the seal of the king. It is difficult to find a text with a royal grant confirmed by oath. There is a Hittite text in which king Hattusilis rewards a faithful retainer and promises that his descendants will keep him in favor, and several gods are in-

3. Jean Nougayrol, Le palais royal d'Ugarit, vol. 3 (Paris, 1955), p. 50, no. 16.275. Restorations have not been marked in the translation.

voked as witnesses. Even so, there is no explicit self-curse, which is the essence of an oath, and it remains uncertain whether there was an exact parallel, on the human level, to the type of agreement we are considering.

There is evidence, however, that covenants with gods other than Yahweh had this nature, that is, that the god promised protection and help to those in covenant with him. "We have made a covenant with Death, and we have concluded a pact with Sheol. When the overwhelming scourge passes, it will not come upon us" (Isaiah 28:15). Plainly the content of this covenant with Death was all in favor of the human partners; in time of calamity they would not be touched. "Death" is capitalized here to make it plain that he was a god, as is demonstrated by the Ugaritic epics. It is interesting to observe that this covenant with a god is, in effect, an agreement that the god will have nothing to do with the human partner! Whether we consider this an attractive faith or not, we may be grateful for such a clear statement of the "Covenant with Death" theology. It permits us to see how easily a covenant in which a god is bound lends itself to use as a shield against the deity's power. Even without other evidence, we would assume that the prophet Isaiah is here reporting authentic heathen conceptions, but we need not merely assume it for there is explicit evidence in an eighth-century B.C. incantation against demons: "The house I enter you [the demons] shall not enter, and the court I tread you shall not tread, for Ashur has made an everlasting covenant with us. He made it with us, and so did all the gods . . . ."

Whatever the ultimate source of the sort of covenant associated with Noah and Abraham, it was on such traditions that David and those about him drew to formulate the idea of a divine covenant in favor of his dynasty. Put in that way, it may sound hypocritical and cynical, a deliberate manipulation of religious feeling in favor of the crown, but it is not my intention to present it as such. It is quite possible, even probable, that David and those of his opinion were perfectly sincere and that they had quite genuine visions and auditions concerning the divine election of David and his line, influenced by the conviction that a strong king and an orderly succession to the throne was necessary for the survival and prosperity of God's people. At any rate, we have widespread attestation of the belief in a covenant with David. Once again, we meet the troublesome problem of dating these materials, and we have no assurance that any of them come from the days of David himself. We will have to reckon with the probability that the texts to be quoted here give us the Davidic covenant in later and somewhat modified versions. We can, however, reasonably suppose that the idea itself is old and that our texts give us a fairly undistorted view of it.

An early attestation is in the so-called Last Words of David, a poem that may well be from David's time since it is full of grammatical archaisms and ancient names for God. Like other ancient biblical poems, it is also bafflingly obscure in places, and one suspects that here and there the text is corrupt. It must be understood that the translation given here is somewhat adventurous. All the same, the lines about the covenant with David are quite clear.

Oracle of David, the son of Jesse,
　　Oracle of the hero whom the Most High exalted,
The anointed of the God of Jacob,
　　The favorite of the Protector of Israel.
The spirit of the Lord spake by me,
　　And His word was on my tongue.
The God of Israel said,
　　To me spake the Mountain of Israel:
"Rule over men righteously,
　　Rule in the fear of God"
　　　　　　　　． ． ．

For my house is truly legitimate before God [4]
For he made an eternal covenant with me,
Arranged in all points and observed (II Samuel 23:1–5).

Not a great deal is clear from this poem except the one major point: David and his house are the favorites of God, and this takes the form of a divine covenant in David's favor, an "eternal covenant."

The following account of the covenant with David is fuller. As its opening sentences show, it is laid in the time when he was enjoying a period of peace after the struggles that brought him to the throne.

> Now as the king was living in his palace, and Yahweh had given him relief from all his enemies round about, he said to Nathan the prophet: "See here, I live in a house of cedar, while the ark of God lives under a tent." So Nathan said to the king: "Whatever you have in mind, go and do it, for Yahweh is with you." Then that very night, the word of Yahweh came to Nathan: "Go say to my servant David, 'Thus says the Lord: Would you build me a house to live in, when I have not lived in a house from the time I brought the Israelites up from Egypt unto this day, but have been going about in a tent, and in a tabernacle? Wherever I went along with all the Israelites, did I speak one word to any of the judges of Israel, whom I commanded to shepherd my people Israel, saying, Why have you not built me a house of cedar? So now this is what you shall say to my servant David. Thus says Yahweh Sabaoth: I took you from the fold, from following the flock, to be a commander (*nagid*) over my people Israel, and I was with you wherever you went, and I cut down all your enemies before you, and I made a great name for you, a name like any of the great men of the earth. I will make a place for my people Israel, and I will plant it and it shall dwell in its own place, and it will not move again, nor shall perverse men again afflict it as they did at first, from the time that I gave commands to the judges over my people Israel to the time when I gave you relief from all your enemies. And Yahweh tells you that Yahweh will make you a house! When

4. This translation is based on taking *lo'* as asseverative, not negative, and *ken* as meaning "rightful, legitimate," a meaning which Akkadian *kinu* has in some contexts.

your days are done, and you lie down with your fathers, I
will raise up after you one of your descendants, one who comes
from your loins, and I will establish his rule. He will build a
house for my name, and I will establish the throne of his
kingship forever. I will be his father, and he will be my son.
When he does wrong, I will correct him by the rod of men,
with blows given by the sons of men, but my loyalty will not
turn away from him, as I turned it away from Saul, whom
I removed from before you. But your house and kingship shall
be firmly fixed forever before me. Your throne shall be established forever.' " So Nathan spoke to David, telling all these
things, this whole revelation (II Samuel 7:1–17).

We may omit David's grateful prayer for the most part,
but we should cite the following: "You have established your
people Israel as your people forever, and you, Yahweh, have
become their God. And now, Yahweh, [my] god, this thing
which you have spoken about your servant and his dynasty,
make it stand forever, and do as you have spoken" (7:24–25).
And a bit farther along: "Now, my Lord, Yahweh, you are
God, whose words are reliable, and you have promised [liter-
ally, "spoken"] to your servant this pact of friendship" (7:28).

The first point of interest is the manner in which this
covenant is communicated—for our purposes it makes no
great difference whether this is really what happened in
David's time, or whether this is simply the story that was
circulated somewhat later. The covenant is transmitted
through a prophet. This helps explain how the idea of a
covenant with the king gained acceptance and publicity. Even
under the tribal league the prophets had enjoyed a popular
reputation as spokesmen for Yahweh. David's choice by
God, then, is announced with the authority of one such
prestigious figure, Nathan. Even so, we should note that we
do not have completely satisfactory evidence as to how the
covenant with the king was publicized. We have seen that the
Sinai covenant was by nature a public transaction, and so
were the repetitions and renewals of this covenant which

followed. Furthermore, this older covenant figured largely in the liturgy at the pilgrimage shrine and was part of the worship carried on at home. We may suppose that not only Nathan but also other court prophets delivered public oracles regarding God's choice of David's line, and the fact that a number of psalms refer to the covenant with David demonstrates that the official cultus at the Jerusalem temple included prayer for the anointed of the Lord. Coronations must have been impressive ceremonies and would have helped inculcate the covenant theory on the populace. However it happened, the idea gained wide currency. Yet it seems just to say that this remains a theory by comparison with the Sinai covenant. At least in early days, before the monarchy, the covenant with God was something in which every family had participated, if only in liturgical repetition. Yahweh's covenant with the king was something people heard about, not something they enacted.

What follows the introduction is very much along the lines of the pacts of God with Noah and Abraham: a promise by God with no corresponding obligation on the monarch. Beyond this generality, however, some of the details are fascinating. When the oracle says: "I *took* you from the fold [italics mine], from following the flock, to be a commander (*nagid*) over my people Israel," it is evident that we are dealing with a carefully couched political document, a charter for royalty which makes all the proper bows to democratic sentiment. The ideal in early Israel was what might be called the Abe Lincoln ideal, from log cabin to White House, only with a deeper theoretical basis. Since only Yahweh was king, human leaders were not constituted permanent possessors of authority but were those whom Yahweh chose when and as it pleased him, and Yahweh's glory was shown most when he raised up the obscure and gave victory through them. "He hath put down the mighty from their seats, and exalted them of low degree." As stated above, there was at first a certain reserve about use of royal titles, and the oracle respects this by calling David *nagid*, that is, *imperator*, "commander." When Amos describes his call to be a prophet, it is in almost identical terms: "I was no prophet, nor a member of a prophetic group, for I was a herdsman, and a tender of sycamore figs. But Yahweh *took me* [italics mine] from following the flock . . ." (Amos 7:15). This is, then, the proper way for an inspired, charismatic figure to appear on the scene—"God took me . . . ."—and David is thus presented as the ideal leader of the theocracy, the consummation of what a "judge" should be, while in the very act of substituting hereditary monarchy for theocracy. Again the analogy of Rome comes to mind: the beginning of the Empire coincides with the year when "the republic was restored."

If God is in league with the house of David, just what does this mean? One most significant way in which the content of this covenant is expressed lies in the words, "I will be his father, and he will be my son." The king is God's adopted son. This is intriguingly vague, especially when considered in the light of the other nations. In Egypt, the king was the son of a god and himself divine. He was the human manifestation of the divine power that ruled all things. In Mesopotamia and in the Canaanite city-states kings were less often deified, and still less often were they regarded as gods during their lifetime. So if Israel made herself a king "like all the nations," there was a variety of models for an understanding of "He shall be my son." We should be reminded that it is not at all common in the Hebrew Bible for men to be called "sons of God," however current such language became in the New Testament and later Christian writings. In Hebrew and its sister languages, "sons of god" ordinarily means "gods, divine beings," since "son of" is a Semitic idiom for membership in a certain class. When the psalm quotes the "decree" of God in favor of the king: "You are my son, today I have begotten you" (2:7), it is pushing royal claims to the limit. There is an obvious reserve, within Israel, at spelling out the implications of such a formula, and it is never carried to a point that would contradict the uniqueness of Yahweh's godhead. At the same time, the covenant with the king, especially when defined as the divine sonship of the king, elevated the monarch above common humanity. In a late biblical book, the king of Judah is called "the anointed of the Lord, the breath of our nostrils" (Lamentations 4:20), a bit of hyperbole which echoes, probably by direct descent, the language that fawning vassals used in the Amarna correspondence as an address to Pharaoh.

This covenant is such that even wrongdoing cannot break it. The nation may suffer if the king is wicked, for God will chastise them as a father beats an erring son. But the oath of God will stand, even so! There could not be any clearer evidence of the great gulf that is fixed between this and the intention of the Sinai covenant, where the stress is on Israel's responsibility. The statement here, shaped no doubt by Israel's experience of what David did to Uriah, of Solomon's apostasies, and so on, asserts that God is bound to this promise no matter what. But at the same time, although this contrasts sharply with Sinai, there is a transfer from the older covenant pattern. If the older covenant spoke of blessings for obedience and curses for disobedience on the part of all Israel, this covenant now strikes the motif that Israel's history will henceforth be determined by the character of her king.

Another evidence of an attempt at accommodation to Israel's older faith lies in David's prayer of thanks, part of which is quoted above. David recites a bit of the sacred covenant history and concludes with the standard summing-up of the covenant: Israel is Yahweh's people, Yahweh is God of

Israel. Now, he says, establish your covenant with me. This is not a real integration of the royal covenant with the older pattern; it simply tacks the new onto the old and does nothing at all to resolve the inherent tension between the two ideas. Yet it is effective, probably more effective than any real attempt at solving the difficulty. The tension is simply ignored; the story is told to give the impression that there is no problem and as though the present transaction with David follows naturally on what happened at Sinai. The final bit of David's prayer has been translated above to make the point that this oracle to David is specifically called a "covenant" or "pact," though a different word is used here, not the ordinary *berit* but *tobah*. Etymologically related words are often used outside the Bible for "friendly relations established by treaty," and there are several passages in the Old Testament where the Hebrew word may now be recognized as having this sense.[5]

Psalm 89 gives a more detailed poetic expression of the theory.

I would sing of (your) loyalty, Yahweh,
    To all generations I would make known your faithfulness.
With your own mouth you declared:
"Forever shall loyalty be built up,
    Faithfulness shall be fixed firm in heaven.
For lo, I have made a pact with my chosen one,
    I have sworn to David, my servant.
'Forever will I establish your descendants,
    And I will build your throne for all generations.' "
(In) the heavens they shall praise your promise, Yahweh,
    Even your faithfulness in the assembly of the Holy Ones.
For who in the sky can compare with Yahweh?
    Of the gods, who is like Yahweh?
God inspires terror in the counsel of the Holy Ones,

5. See Delbert R. Hillers, "A Note on Some Treaty Terminology in the Old Testament," *Bulletin of the American Schools of Oriental Research*, 176 (December, 1964): 46–47, for other biblical occurrences of this term and for references to earlier studies by William L. Moran.

He is great and feared above all round about him.
Yahweh God of Sabaoth, who is like you?

　　. . .

You rule over the raging of Sea,
　　When his waves toss, you calm them.
You crushed Rahab like one slain,
　　By your mighty arm you have scattered your enemies.
The heavens are yours, and so is the earth,
　　The world and what is in it, you have founded.
You created Zaphon and Amana;
　　Tabor and Hermon exult at your name
To you belongs a mighty arm.
　　Your hand is strong, your right hand is exalted.
On right and justice your throne stands,
　　Loyalty and faithfulness are your retainers.
Happy the people who know the victory cry;
　　Yahweh, they will walk in the light of your face.
In your name they will rejoice all day long,
　　And be exalted at your righteousness.
For you are our mighty glory;
　　By your favor you will lift up our horn.
For it is Yahweh who is our protector,
　　The Holy One of Israel who is our King.

Then you spoke in a vision to the faithful and said:
"I have preferred a youth above warriors,
　　I have raised up a young hero out of the host.
I have found David, my servant;
　　With my holy oil I have anointed him.
With him will my hand abide firm,
　　Yes, my arm will strengthen him.
No enemy will deceive him,
　　No wicked person afflict him.
I will beat his foes from before him,
　　And repulse those that hate him.
My faith and loyalty will belong to him
　　And his horn will be high by my name.
I will put his hand on the Sea,
　　His right hand on the Rivers.
He will call me: 'You are my father,
　　My God, my saving mountain.'
And I will make him the first-born,

High up above the kings of the earth.
Forever I will keep faith with him;
    My covenant with him will be reliable.
I will make his line endure forever,
    And his throne last as long as the heavens.
Should his sons leave my law,
    And not live by my just orders,
If they profane my statutes
    And do not keep my commandments,
I will punish their rebellion with a rod
    And their iniquity with beatings.
But I will not break faith with him
    And I will not be false to my promise.
I will not profane my covenant
    I will not change what has gone forth from my lips.
I swore once, by my holiness:
    'I will not lie to David.
His line shall endure forever,
    His throne be like the sun before me,
Like the moon, established forever,
    A reliable ordinance in the sky.' "

But you have rejected and cast off,
    You have shown anger toward your anointed one.
You have spurned the covenant of your servant,
    Cast his diadem to earth, profaned.
You have broken down all his walls,
    Have made his fortresses into ruins.
All passersby have despoiled him,
    Neighbors have despised him.
You have raised his enemies' right hand,
    You have made his foes happy.
You have turned back the edge of his sword,
    You have not let him stand and fight.
You have broken his glorious sceptre,
    You have toppled his throne to the ground.
You have shortened the days of his youth,
    You have clothed him in frustration.
How long will you hide, Yahweh, forever?
    How long will your wrath burn like fire?
Remember . . . .

          . . .

What man can live and not see death,
    Can deliver himself from the power of Sheol?
Where is the loyalty you showed at first, O Lord?
    What you swore to David by your own faithfulness?
Remember, Yahweh, how your servant has borne reproach,
    How he has borne in his bosom strife with the nations,
How your enemies have reviled, Yahweh,
    Have reviled (with) insults your anointed.[6]

Hebrew poems are ordinarily not notable for logical organization, but this is exceptional, for it follows a carefully conceived plan and the fundamental unity of theme and imagery becomes even more apparent with study. It adds little to the actual ideas we have looked at in II Samuel 7, but it adds a great deal of the setting, of the literary and religious associations that collected about the covenant with the house of David. The opening verses announce the theme: God's faithfulness to David. There follows a lengthy praise of God's incomparable power in creation, his dominion over the world of nature. This may seem at first like a digression, but it is tied to the main theme on at least three levels. The most obvious might be called the level of piety. Since the psalm turns out to be a petition for help, a plea for God to keep his promise, any possible crassness of this appeal, any danger of reducing God's dignity by having to remind him of an obligation, is neutralized by an initial expression of the immeasurable grandeur of his power. At a deeper level, this hymning of God who created and established all things, firmly and unshakably, meshes with the theme that the rule of David's line is an order of creation, like the sun,

6. The Hebrew text of this psalm is generally clear, but there are a few difficult lines. I have omitted several, as marked; in other cases Ugaritic evidence has suggested the rendering given. For detailed philological comment, see Mitchell Dahood, *Psalms II: 50–100*, The Anchor Bible, vol. 17 (Garden City, N. Y., 1968), which is the source of my translation at some points.

eternal as the heavens, established like the moon, an eternal ordinance in the heavens. At a still subtler level there is correspondence in the mythological motifs introduced. The account of Yahweh's creation is full of themes occurring in Canaanite and Babylonian mythology: the counsel of gods ("the holy ones"), their terror at a greater god, the victory of God over the Sea and its monsters at the beginning of all things, and the creation of heaven and earth and the sacred mountains (originally themselves gods, Zaphon being the Canaanite Olympus). Thus the poet enriches his language with originally mythological themes, and these themes recur when it is time to talk of David: the lines about David's irresistible victories over his enemies, and those which speak of setting his hand on the Sea (Hebrew Yam) and his right hand on the River (Naharot), are reminiscent, down to the very words, of the god Baal's victory over his enemy, Sea (Yam), whose other name is River (Nahar). The lines about God as the king's father, the king as God's first-born, "High up above the kings of the earth," touch—again, quite discreetly —on themes of the divine origin of heroes, the favoring of one child as first-born by a god. I dwell on these last two points, imagery of creation, the ties of this imagery to mythology, to emphasize the contrast to the thought-world associated with the Sinai covenant. There we are in the realm of human history, and God's bond to his people is based on the way he has shown them his favor in their past. In the sacred history we hear of the exodus and of victories over such concrete figures as Og, king of Bashan, and Sihon, king of the Amorites. With David's covenant we are in a different world. God makes himself known in creation, in his primeval victory over chaos and establishment of the order of this world, and his bond to the people Israel is through this line of monarchs, which is itself part of the order of creation and links heaven and earth. The bond made at Sinai is precarious, fragile as the people's faith; the bond with David is as firm as the sun and moon, as reliable as God.

The next passages of the psalm follow logically on the foregoing. The people are experiencing defeat and can only conclude that for some mysterious reason God has spurned his covenant with the king. The only hope is that God will correct things again; it is up to Yahweh to "remember." There is no confession of sin on the part of king or people; there is an acknowledgment of human frailty, but this seems to mean primarily that human flesh can stand only so much of this trouble—"how long, Yahweh?"

It is not to be imagined that this extremely high theory of the monarchy was held always, everywhere, and by everyone. After Solomon's death the larger section of the nation, the ten northern tribes, seceded and became a separate kingdom. The grounds for this withdrawal were the autocratic exactions which Solomon had demanded and which his son was threatening to increase. It was a conservative revolution, and it is worth noting how a new king was chosen for the North. According to I Kings, Jeroboam had been in exile but returned when he heard of the division of the kingdom. "When all Israel heard that Jeroboam had returned, they sent a message and invited him to the assembly, and made him king over all Israel. No one followed the house of David except the tribe of Judah, all by itself" (12:20). The key term here is "assembly" (Hebrew ʿedah), the name for the assembly of tribal representatives under the pre-monarchic league. Old tradition comes to life again at this point, and though the assembly appoints a king, it is unthinkable that they meant to have the same kind of king as the sons of David were claiming to be. In particular, these northerners evidently did not give complete assent to a hereditary principle, for though Judah is ruled throughout her history by one dynasty, no royal line managed to maintain itself for more than a couple of generations in the north. Unfortunately, we do not have as much information about affairs in the northern kingdom as we would like, since the Bible was compiled in the southern kingdom, Judah, and is on the whole more interested in affairs there. But there is enough evidence to permit us to say that a divine covenant with the king was not a firm part of the faith up north, and when from time to time a conservative, republican tradition stirs in the south, we may reasonably inquire whether influence from the north was behind it.

Even with these reservations, however, the dominant idea in Judah, from David's time on, was that God had promised the land to Abraham by covenant and in a parallel way had promised dominion to the line of David. Through this divinely ordained king would come the fruits of a world in harmony. According to Psalm 72, the king "comes down like rain on the new-mown land, like showers that sprinkle the earth," and the psalmist adds the prayer:

Long may he live!
  May gold of Sheba be given him!
Let constant prayer for him be made,
  Let them bless him the livelong day.
May there be plenty of grain in the land,
  May it wave on top of the hills.
May its fruit blossom like Lebanon.

CHAPTER SIX

"THEREFORE I WILL PUNISH YOU"

The topic of this chapter is "the covenant and the prophets," a subject that will not yield to frontal assault. A traditional line of approach to prophetic use of the covenant idea has been to locate all the passages where the prophets use the word "covenant" and then to write up the results on that basis. Since there are very few passages where the earlier prophets use the word, the conclusion is predictable: "covenant" occupied a very minor place in prophetic thought. If one thought of the covenant idea as preceding the days of the eighth-century prophets, then one could hold that they had largely abandoned the old idea; if one held that the covenant idea developed later, then one could cite the prophetic silence as proving that they did not know of a covenant between God and his people. Recent studies, however, show that a very different estimate results from an indirect approach and that out of such varied materials as the Hebrew verb "to know," a literary pattern known as the lawsuit of God, and a handful of ancient curses we can construct a truer picture of what "covenant" meant to the prophets of Israel.

The Hebrew verb "to know," yadaʿ, is a peculiarly flexible word which is used in senses ranging from "to understand" to "to sleep with a woman." It is no wonder, then, that the religious use of such a protean term causes some problems. When the Old Testament speaks of the knowledge of God, does it mean acquaintance with him, intellectual understanding of his being, or which of a still wider range of possibilities? And what does it mean when Yahweh is said to *know*

Israel? "Hear this word which Yahweh has spoken against you, O Israelites, Against the whole family which I brought up from the land of Egypt: You only have I known of all the families on earth. Therefore I will punish you for all your iniquities." These words of Amos (3:1–2) are introduced in such a way that it is evident they were delivered with an awful solemnity. But what do they mean? In what sense is it true that Yahweh has known only Israel, and why the "Therefore"? What is the logical connection between God's knowledge of Israel and her doom?

It is only very recently that it has become clear that we have here a usage of "know" borrowed from international relations. Herbert B. Huffmon was the first to point out that Near Eastern kings use "to know" (in both Hittite and Akkadian texts) in two technical legal senses: to recognize as legitimate suzerain or vassal, and to recognize treaty stipulations as binding.[1] Thus "the Sun," the great king of the Hittites, writes in a treaty with Huqqanas: "And you, Huqqanas, 'know' only the Sun regarding lordship. Moreover, do not 'know' another lord! 'Know' the Sun alone!" "Know" has been retained here, to make the linguistic point under discussion, but it is clear that the term might have been translated "recognize," or almost "be subject, loyal to." In a different treaty, another Hittite king assures a vassal that he will protect his vassal should some underling rebel against him: "As he (the rebel) is an enemy to you, even so is he an enemy to the Sun; (and) I, the Sun, will know only you." Here again "recognize" would be a closer English equivalent. Similar uses of "to know" have been identified in the Amarna letters, a body of correspondence mostly written by Palestinian subject-kings to their Egyptian overlords in the fifteenth and

1. See his "The Treaty Background of Hebrew Yadaʿ," *Bulletin of the American Schools of Oriental Research*, 181 (February, 1966): 31–37, on which the discussion here is based.

fourteenth centuries B.C., the language being a barbarous Akkadian, and in the much earlier Mari letters: "Apart from Yasmah-Addu, the king our lord, we do not recognize another king." A letter from Ugarit (thirteenth century B.C.), even though slightly damaged, is noteworthy in this respect because the language, Ugaritic prose, is in this passage nearly identical to biblical Hebrew: "Now [you belong?] to the Sun, your lord; You are his property. Now, [how is it that] you do not recognize the Sun, your lord? Why have you not come to me, the Sun, your lord, for a year, indeed, for two years?" [2] Thus verbs meaning "to know" in ordinary contexts were used for "to recognize," "be loyal to," in the vocabulary of international relations over a wide range of the ancient world, and the reader will anticipate the significance of this for the prophets.

"You only have I known of all the families on earth. Therefore I will punish you for all your iniquities." Amos' words are no longer mysterious. Yahweh had recognized only Israel as his legitimate servants; only to them had he granted the covenant. "Therefore," since this sort of covenant involves obligations and since they had not fulfilled them, "I will punish you for all your iniquities." Hosea uses "know" in the same way (13:4–5): "I am Yahweh, your God, from the land of Egypt, and you shall not recognize [know] any God but me. There is no other savior. And I acknowledged you [knew you] as mine in the wilderness, in the land of drought." Jeremiah speaks in the same way when describing a future repentance of the people (24:7): "Then I will give them a heart to know that I am Yahweh, and they shall be my people, and I will be their God." That this kind of knowledge is closely related to the people's

2. The last two passages are dealt with in Herbert B. Huffmon and Simon B. Parker, "A Further Note on the Treaty Background of Hebrew Yadaʿ," ibid., 184 (December, 1966): 36–38.

conduct is evident from another passage in Jeremiah (22:15–16). The prophet is indicting the reigning monarch for thinking that being king is merely a matter of having a splendid palace: "Will striving to excel in cedar make you a king? Your father ate and drank, and did justice and right, and it was well with him. He judged the cause of the poor and the needy . . . . Is not that knowing me?" Hosea makes the same connection (4:1–2): "Hear the word of Yahweh, O Israelites, for Yahweh has a lawsuit against the inhabitants of the land. For there is no faithfulness, or loyalty, or knowledge of God in the land. They have broken out in cursing, cheating, murder, thieving, and adultery, and spilt blood touches blood." Hosea's list is very much like the Ten Commandments, down to the specific words used. A considerable number of comparable passages could be cited, both in the books of the prophets and in the rest of the Old Testament. This is, of course, not the only sense in which "know" is used, but as a religious term yada' often has this sense.

"To make dictionaries is dull work," Samuel Johnson observed, and perhaps the above essay at defining a Hebrew word proves his contention, but the lexical point seems important to me for two reasons. The first is simply because of the gain in understanding what the Old Testament means by "knowing God." This kind of knowledge of God is primarily unmystical and unintellectual. It is not acquired by protracted study or contemplation, or by admission to the secrets of some esoteric lore. Instead it is shown in a life of performance of God's will, a will that is easily understood and common knowledge. The second outcome of our consideration of the word "to know" is that we see a connection between prophetic language and thought and the terminology associated with treaty relationships. Even if the word "covenant" is not prominently on display in their writings, the complex of ideas associated with covenant is present as an invisible framework, in this case forming the foundation for one of their principal concerns, the knowledge of God.

From concern for a single term, we now move to treatment of a literary form found in a number of the prophetic books, the so-called lawsuit of God, or covenant lawsuit. Before doing so, it is good to have clearly in mind what is meant by "form" in this connection, and why this mode of study is followed. The books of Israel's prophets are among the most difficult in the Old Testament, and probably among the most difficult books ever written. The oracles are often tantalizingly brief and are for the most part couched in a highly concentrated poetic language and joined together with no obvious regard for logical or chronological sequence. The reader, even with the best will in the world, is often at a loss to tell where an individual speech begins or ends and is frequently left to guess from vague hints within an oracle when and where it was delivered—and by which prophet, for critical study has made it evident that not everything in a given prophetic book comes from the man whose name it bears. In recent decades scholars have made some progress with this daunting material by paying special attention to the forms of composition which the prophets used. It must be understood that these are not forms comparable to, let us say, the sonnet, that is, a literary unit with a fixed number of lines, a certain rhyme-scheme, and so on. When scholars speak of "forms" they mean the separate genres of composition, exhibiting certain typical themes, arranged in a more or less fixed pattern. The length of each element in a complex form is not fixed, nor is the poetic meter, which varies. When such a form has been identified, the attempt is made to define the situation for which it was used, not in the sense of fixing the precise moment when a given prophet used it, which is usually impossible, but of discovering the typical, recurring circumstances to which a given form was addressed. Even this more modest aim is rarely achieved with certainty, which is not surprising—could a later age reconstruct from the bare lyrics the peculiar circumstances in our own society in which popular love-songs are written and sung? But some of the results are relatively reliable, and the lawsuit of God, which concerns us, is one form of prophetic speech about which there is a fair measure of general agreement.

The form derives its name from its central feature: Yahweh is depicted as taking his people to court. Aside from this central metaphor there are a number of other more or less common features that make it possible to isolate the type and study it separately. There is often a call to heaven and earth, or to the mountains and hills, to serve as witnesses, and there is a summons to the defendant, Israel. Yahweh states his case, often brushing aside possible defenses which the people might advance, and pronounces their guilt, or the sentence. These "lawsuit" addresses have been identified in Deuteronomy 32, the "Song of Moses," which is a very long example, and Isaiah 1:2–3, a very short one, and elsewhere, but for our purposes it may suffice to study two others, of moderate length, beginning with Micah 6:1-8.

> Hear now what Yahweh is saying:
> "Arise, plead before the mountains,
>   And let the hills hear your voice."
> O mountains, hear the suit of Yahweh,
>   Ye eternal foundations of the earth,
> For Yahweh has a suit against his people,
>   He would contest with Israel.
> "O my people, what have I done to you,
>   How have I wearied you? Answer me!
> For I brought you up from the land of Egypt,
>   And from the house of bondage I redeemed you.
> I sent before you Moses,
>   Aaron and Miriam.
> O my people, recall now the plot
>   Of Balak the king of Moab,

And the response he obtained
   From Balaam the son of Beor . . .
[something has been dropped from the text]
   From Shittim to Gilgal,
That you may acknowledge [know] the righteous deeds of
   Yahweh!"
"With what can I come before Yahweh,
   Bow to God on high?
Shall I come before him with burnt-offerings
   With calves a year old?
Would Yahweh be pleased with thousands of rams
   With ten thousands of rivers of oil?
Can I give my first born for my rebellion
   The fruit of my loins for my sin?"
"He has shown you, man, what is good.
   Yahweh seeks nothing from you
Except that you do justice, love faithfulness,
   And walk humbly with your God."

Jeremiah's contribution in this form is as follows (2:4–13):

Hear the word of Yahweh, O house of Jacob,
   And all the clans of the house of Israel.
Thus say Yahweh:
"What did your fathers find wrong with me,
   That they went away from me
And followed nothings,
   And themselves became nothing?
They did not say, 'Where is Yahweh,
   Who brought us up from the land of Egypt,
Who led us in the wilderness
   In the land of steppes and holes,
In the land of drought and darkness,
   The land uncrossed by man
   Where no human dwells.'
I brought you to a garden-land,
   To eat its fruits and riches,
But you went in and defiled my land,
   And made my heritage an abomination.
The priests did not say,
   'Where is Yahweh?'
And those in charge of instruction did not acknowledge [know]
   me,
   And the shepherds rebelled against me.

The prophets prophesied by Baal
And followed futilities.
Therefore I will surely bring suit against you
    (oracle of Yahweh),
With your children's children I will contend.
For pass over to the shores of Cyprus and see,
    Send to Arabia and inquire carefully,
Has any nation ever changed its gods,
    Even though they were no-gods?
But my people has changed its glory
    For futility.
Be appalled at this, O heavens,
    Be utterly aghast, O dry land (oracle of Yahweh),
For my people have done two evil things,
    They have forsaken me,
The spring of fresh water,
    To hew them out cisterns,
Broken cisterns that will not hold water!"

As different as these two are in imagery and tone, the basic similarity is evident, and as we review them, we will concentrate on those elements that mark this form as connected with the covenant.[3] In both there is an appeal to certain natural elements to serve in some capacity, whether as witnesses or judges or executioners is not immediately clear. In Micah it is "mountains" and "the hills," and in Jeremiah it is "Be appalled at this, O heavens" (in the parallel line we would expect "O earth" and I have restored "dry land," simply guessing at the Hebrew word in a line that is slightly corrupt textually). In other "lawsuits" the appeal is: "Hear O heavens, and give ear, O earth" (Isaiah 1:2); "Give

3. Hugo Gressmann and Hermann Gunkel identified the lawsuit as a special literary form in important early studies; the term "covenant lawsuit" was first applied by Herbert B. Huffmon, "The Covenant Lawsuit in the Prophets," *Journal of Biblical Literature*, 78 (1959): 285–95. A more recent study, especially devoted to Deuteronomy 32, is "The Lawsuit of God" by G. Ernest Wright, in *Israel's Prophetic Heritage*, ed. Bernhard W. Anderson and Walter Harrelson (New York, 1962), pp. 26–67. The last two studies form the principal basis for the treatment here.

ear, O heavens, that I may speak, and let the earth hear the words of my mouth" (Deuteronomy 32:1). It was George Mendenhall who first pointed out that this is a parallel to the international treaties, in which heaven and earth, mountains and hills, and other portions of the cosmos are invoked as witnesses. The parallel is made more impressive when we consider that in the Old Testament this appeal to heaven and earth is regularly used in a context connected with the covenant, either in this lawsuit form or in passages that specifically have to do with the covenant, and its keeping, such as Deuteronomy 4:25–26: "If you beget sons and grandsons and grow old in the land, and become corrupt and make an image, any sort of likeness, and do evil in the sight of Yahweh your god, and provoke him, I adjure you today by heaven and earth that you will soon utterly perish from the land." Similarly, outside the Bible, appeal to heaven and earth as witnesses is practically limited to treaties. It is a standard feature of the second-millennium Hittite treaties, is attested at Ugarit, recurs in a different form in one of the Aramaic Sefire treaties (eighth century B.C.), and stands in Hannibal's treaty with Philip V of Macedon (235 B.C.), which, although preserved only in Greek, is a translation of a Punic original. It was stated in an earlier chapter that the list of divine witnesses is not part of the form of the covenant with God, for an obvious reason. Even so, here we have a case where the prophets retain a vestige of the old form as a literary device. I say "old form" because it is likely that the motif entered Israelite religious and literary tradition early rather than late. The Song of Moses, Deuteronomy 32, which contains an invocation of heaven and earth, is itself a relatively early composition, and the inclusion of these witnesses is not attested in extra-biblical texts from the Near East past the eighth century B.C. Later Assyrian treaties do not have it. (I am discounting Hannibal's treaty because it seems likely that Carthaginian legal practices and forms were introduced in North Africa at the founding of this Phoenician colony and that this is an example of the familiar situation in which a provincial, outlying group or colony preserves old forms longer than the metropolis or homeland.)

Although we may be fairly certain about the ultimate source of this biblical appeal to heaven and earth, it is not so easy to say what the biblical writers meant by it, or how much importance they attached to it. Some, notably G. Ernest Wright, have supposed that heaven and earth, being originally gods, are in the Bible invoked as members of Yahweh's council. In support of this one can gather a fair body of evidence that for all Israel's monotheism, she did not insist that Yahweh ruled entirely alone but thought of him as surrounded by "the sons of God," that is, other heavenly beings. To paraphrase the old song, One was One, but not all alone. If this view is correct, then the lawsuit of God is conceived of as conducted before his divine council. In the opinion of others, the appeal to heaven and earth is a bit of literary machinery, which we must not press too far for information about Israel's actual religious beliefs. However one weighs the evidence, the prophets reveal in this detail their contact with the language of treaties, however long and complicated the course of tradition through which it reached them.

We may deal more briefly with other covenant elements in these lawsuits. Yahweh's complaint is made, in both the cases quoted, on the basis of history, and we may rightly call it covenant history. For the beginning is with exodus, and we hear of the frustration of Balaam's oracles and of the gift of the land. These events, Micah says, should have led the people to "acknowledge ["know," yada°] the righteous deeds of Yahweh." The indictment is implied in Micah, explicit in Jeremiah. Micah's version permits us to conclude only that the people were tired of Yahwism, were not doing justice, keeping faith, and walking humbly with God. Jere- miah uses language more easily identified as associated with the covenant: "Those in charge of instruction did not ac- knowledge [yada°] me, and the shepherds [that is, the kings] rebelled against me." The verb I have translated as "rebel" is originally a political term, and its use in the religious vocabulary is rooted in the political metaphor at the bottom of so much of the religion. With the extravagant offer of sacrifices, put in the mouth of a spokesman for the people, Micah makes a point which is expressed more succinctly by Hosea: "I desire loyalty, not sacrifice, and knowledge of God more than burnt-offerings" (Hosea 6:6). In other words, even the most lavish sacrificial ritual cannot replace fidelity to the covenant and its Lord, so the people cannot point to their observance of cultic forms as a substitute for obedience. Thus the sentence is "Guilty." Micah puts it in a memo- rable, terse formulation with echoes of the language associ- ated with the covenant. God's first inescapable requirement is that the Israelites do "justice," Hebrew mishpat, a common term for the legal norms demanded by the covenant. The next phrase is practically untranslatable; the Israelites should love "hesed." Hesed is the quality one wants in a partner to an alliance, hence it involves loyalty above all. But it is more than just abiding by the letter of what one is legally required to do. It is the quality shown when a man helps a partner who needs it, hence it connotes "kindness, mercy, grace." A good example is the deed of the men of Jabesh Gilead for Saul, their overlord. When the Philistines took Saul's corpse and hung it in contempt from the wall of Beth Shan, the men of Jabesh Gilead came by night, res- cued it, and gave it decent burial. This, as David specifically acknowledged, was "hesed" toward their suzerain Saul, an act of loyalty and kindness above the strict call of duty.

Finally, in Hosea's summary, they are to "walk" humbly with God. Although it would be forced to call this word "walk" technical legal language, since "walk" is a common metaphor for conduct of life, it is worth pointing out that "walk," especially in the phrase "to walk after," is used to describe the relation of a vassal to his lord. Outside the Bible it occurs in the Amarna letters, as William L. Moran has pointed out.[4] Rib-Addi of Byblos writes to Pharaoh of how he had resisted the temptation to join in a conspiracy against Egypt led by the son of Abdiashirta: the people of Byblos had urged him "Walk after [follow] the son of Abdiashirta, and let us make a peace-treaty between us." In sum, the lawsuit form in the prophets deserves the name "covenant lawsuit." The basic idea, the relation between Yahweh and Israel as a bond between partners, and details of formulation all suggest that the prophets were thoroughly familiar with concepts and terms having to do with the covenant.

Readers of European literature scarcely need reminding that authors constantly draw imagery from the Old Testament. When Blake writes: "My heaven is brass, my earth is iron, my moon a clod of clay,"[5] he is echoing the Authorized Version's "Thy heaven that is over thy head shall be brass, and the earth that is under thee shall be iron." If the reader's biblical knowledge is not minute enough to place the quotation, chances are that a helpful editor will supply a footnote: Deuteronomy 28:23. Having reached the biblical fount, both common readers and scholars are apt to be satisfied that they have discovered the original, and of course they are right, in a sense. But one of the pleasant minor outcomes of the recovery of ancient Near Eastern

4. William L. Moran, "The Ancient Near Eastern Background of the Love of God in Deuteronomy," *Catholic Biblical Quarterly*, 25 (1963): 83, n. 35.

5. In *The Four Zoas*.

literature is that we can, in some cases, push the inquiry further and pursue a metaphor to a source preceding the Bible. It is amusing to trace an image like this of Blake's back through the Bible to a Babylonian original and to discover that anything so slight would have survived so long. The pursuit would be little more than a diversion, but for our present purpose it can teach us something about the source of prophetic imagery of doom. For again and again we find that the prophets frame their oracles of woe in terms echoing the curses associated with treaties. Having done so, we have discovered another pointer to the importance of the covenant to the prophets.[6]

The first example will be given with rather full detail, both because it is a clear illustration of the prophets' use of traditional curses and because giving the whole range of biblical evidence will make another important point: much of the prophets' imagery is conventional. Jeremiah 5 depicts the prophet, like an Israelite Diogenes, searching through Jerusalem for one righteous man. Since he does not find even one, he announces doom in Yahweh's name:

> Therefore a lion from the forest shall smite them;
>   A desert wolf shall ravage them.
> A panther is watching over their cities;
>   Everyone who leaves them shall be torn in pieces (5:6).

Commentators have often taken these lines as figurative for the enemies of Judah, but there is no real need to do so. Consider these curses from the long list attached to the first Sefire treaty (eighth century B.C.): "May the gods send every sort of devourer against Arpad and against its people! [May the mo]uth of a snake [eat], the mouth of a scorpion, the mouth of a bear, the mouth of a panther. And may a moth

---

6. For a fuller treatment of curses and their echoes in the prophets, see Delbert R. Hillers, *Treaty-Curses and the Old Testament Prophets* (Rome, 1964).

and a louse and a [. . . become] to it *a serpent's throat!*" [7]
The second Sefire treaty is badly broken at this point, but
the legible portions contain a similar list, adding the lion:
"[And may] the mouth of a lion [eat] and the mouth of
[a . . .] and the mouth of a panther . . . ." Esarhaddon's
treaty with Baal of Tyre (about 677 B.C.) contains a briefer
curse with the same threat: "May Bethel and Anath Bethel
put you at the mercy of a devouring lion." One of the most
significant biblical parallels is in Leviticus 26. Its special
importance derives from the nature of this chapter, for it
is a long list of curses associated with a covenant with Yahweh—it tells what will happen "If you reject my statutes,
and loathe my laws so that you do not perform all my commandments and thus break my covenant." The curse in
verse 22 reads: "Then I will send among you wild animals,
which will make you bereft of children, and destroy your
cattle, and make you few in number and your ways desolate."
Thus just as this curse was traditional in Near Eastern treaties, so we find it attached to a version of Israel's covenant
with Yahweh. If a prophet announces that the curse is
about to be brought on Israel, it is not hard to frame a
hypothesis to cover the situation: the prophets announce
doom in terms known to them and their hearers from the
curses attached to the covenant.

Continuing to examine the "wild animals" curse, we
find other cases where it functions in the same way in the
prophetic literature. The snake, mentioned in the Sefire
treaty, figures in a passage in Jeremiah (8:17): "For behold
I will send among you venomous snakes, against which there
is no incantation. They shall bite you, without any healing."

7. Translated passages from the Sefire inscriptions are given in the
version by Joseph A. Fitzmyer, S.J., *The Aramaic Inscriptions of Sefire*,
Biblica et Orientalia, no. 19 (Rome, 1967), with only slight modifications.

If we find it odd that God is compared to a moth in Hosea (5:12)—"I will be like a moth to Ephraim, and like rot to the house of Judah"—it seems less strange when we consider that the moth is included among the destructive animals in the curses attached to Sefire I. Isaiah 51:8, "For the moth will eat them like a garment, and the clothes moth consume them like wool," is even closer, since the word for moth (sas) is the same as the one used in the Aramaic treaty-curse. Hosea 13:7–8, where God is likened to a lion, a she-bear, and a panther, is another biblical passage whose meaning is illumined by this sort of traditional malediction. Numerous other passages could be cited, but perhaps this many will be enough to introduce the hypothesis that the prophets were often not arbitrary in choosing the lurid figures in which they depicted the wrath to come. They were not indulging a morbid imagination but were fundamentally like lawyers quoting the law: this is just what the covenant curses had said would happen. We can imagine that this contributed a sense of inevitability to their pronouncements.

As a footnote, it is worth recalling that the blessings attached to treaties or covenants may be simply the mirror-images of the curses. Thus it is no surprise to find in the prophecies of weal the same image of wild animals, only reversed: "And I will remove the wild animals from the land" (Leviticus 26:6). "There shall be no lion there, and no violent beast shall come up upon it" (Isaiah 35:9).

We may run more rapidly through other parallels between covenant curses and prophetic imagery. Two treaties threaten rebels with the removal of all joyful sounds from their midst. Thus Sefire I: "Nor may the sound of the lyre be heard in Arpad and among its people." And in the treaty of Ashurnirari V of Assyria (754 B.C.): "May his peasant in the field sing no work-song." Ezekiel echoes the

Sefire curse, even in vocabulary: "And I will put an end to the sound of your songs, and the sound of your lyres shall be heard no more" (26:13). Jeremiah's rhythmic expression of the same thought is familiar: "I will make to cease from the cities of Judah and the streets of Jerusalem the sound of joy and the sound of gladness, the voice of the bridegroom and the voice of the bride" (7:34; 16:9; 25:10; 33:11). On a similar theme, note this curse from the seventh-century treaty of Esarhaddon with his vassals: "May there be no noise of millstone and oven in your houses." Compare Jeremiah's words: "And I will remove from them . . . the sound of the millstones" (Jeremiah 25:10).

One of the most commonly used curses in Akkadian texts is that this or that god should break a man's weapon —most often the bow. Such a curse occurs in the treaties of Esarhaddon with Baal of Tyre and with his other vassals, and in an Aramaic form in Sefire I: "Just as this bow and these arrows are broken, so may Inurta and Hadad break the bow of Mati'el and the bow of his nobles." (Note that this curse was evidently rendered more impressive by an accompanying symbolic act.) Compare Hosea 1:5: "I will break the bow of Israel in the valley of Jezreel," and Jeremiah 49:35: "Behold, I will break the bow of Elam," or Ezekiel 39:3: "I will knock the bow out of your left hand, and I will make your arrows fall from your right hand."

A particularly grisly curse is that men and women should be compelled by famine to eat their own sons and daughters. Of course, this was not a flight of imagination, because both the biblical record and references in Akkadian and Egyptian literature establish that cannibalism occasionally occurred in time of siege. Even so, it is significant that this dire threat stands among the curses of the treaties, in the covenant-curses of both Deuteronomy and Leviticus, and in prophetic doom-oracles. Thus the Ashurnirari treaty: "May they eat the flesh of their sons (and) their daughters and may it taste as good to them as the flesh of a ram or sheep." Esarhaddon rings changes on the theme: "A mother [will close her door] against her own daughter. In your hunger eat the flesh of your sons. Let one eat the flesh of another, let one clothe himself with another's skin. . . . Just as this sheep is cut up and the flesh of her young is put in her mouth, so may he give you to eat in your hunger [the flesh of your wives], the flesh of your brothers, of your sons, and of your daughters. . . . May you eat, while you are alive, your own flesh, and the flesh of your wives, your sons, and your daughters." This inclines toward the repetitive, whereas Deuteronomy 28:53–57 uses circumstantial detail to achieve a more gruesome expression:

> Then you shall eat the fruit of your womb, the flesh of your sons and your daughters which Yahweh your God had given you, in the oppressive siege with which your enemies will press in on you. The tenderest and most sensitive man among you will grudge his brother, even the wife of his bosom, the rest of the children which remain over, so as not to give any of them some of the flesh of his sons, which he shall eat for want of anything else, in the oppressive siege with which your enemies will press in on you at all your gates. The most delicate and sensitive woman among you, the one who would not let the sole of her foot touch the ground, for sheer delicacy and sensitivity, will jealously hoard from her husband and her son and her daughter the afterbirth that comes out from between her legs and the children she bears because she will eat them in secret for want of anything at all, because of the oppressive siege with which your enemies shall press in on you at your gates.

The version in Leviticus 26:29 is more restrained. Jeremiah 19:9 repeats the curse: "I will make them eat the flesh of their sons and the flesh of their daughters. Each shall eat another's flesh." Ezekiel 5:10 is similar: "Therefore fathers shall eat sons in their midst, and sons shall eat their fathers."

The reader is apt to feel that there has been something

too much of this, but it is necessary to see that these parallels are not occasional and scattered, but frequent and striking. We may, however, sum up the rest without quoting. The treaties threaten vassals with having their wives ravished, with having their warriors turned into women, with being left unburied as food for carrion-eaters—this last a most horrible malediction, given the ancients' dread of such a fate. Even a modern might find "We will not bury you" more chilling than "We will bury you." The prophets use all these themes in announcing Yahweh's wrath upon Israel (and, occasionally, on her enemies). One last curse may be cited *in extenso*, as a particularly striking parallel and as the ultimate source of the quotation from Blake with which this section began. Deuteronomy 28:23 has the curse in this form—the Hebrew is metrical: "And your sky o'er your head shall be copper, and (your) ground beneath you iron." One might suspect that this is a traditional curse simply from the fact that Leviticus 26:19 has the same thing in slightly varied form: "I will make your sky like iron, and your ground like copper." Such a suspicion is confirmed by the Esarhaddon vassal treaties, which give the following version: "May they make your ground like iron so that no one can plough [?] it. Just as rain does not fall from a copper sky so may rain and dew not come upon your fields and your meadows." Since none of these is exactly like the others, it is not a case of sheer copying, however we might imagine the lines of dependence to run. But since it is hard to believe that such striking agreement in imagery is due to chance, we must suppose that the biblical writers and the framer of the Esarhaddon treaties were drawing on a common heritage of curses.

What do all these parallels mean for our understanding of the prophets? If we grant that they are striking enough to demand some explanation, then what is a reasonable way of accounting for them? We may well be suspicious of any very simple idea of the prophets' direct dependence on Akkadian treaties. To draw that kind of conclusion would require much more evidence than we possess at present. Where we do have enough evidence to test our hypothesis, the situation turns out to be rather complicated, not simple. There is a curse in a ninth-century Assyrian treaty which calls for a god to "Break the sceptre" of the vassal. This has parallels in Isaiah 14:5: "Yahweh has broken the staff of the wicked, the sceptre of rulers"; in Jeremiah 48:17: "How the mighty staff is broken, the glorious sceptre"; and in several other passages. But before we can conclude that this demonstrates a direct tie between the prophets and a covenant tradition, we must take account of the occurrence of the same curse at the end of the Code of Hammurapi, in a poetic couplet in the Ugaritic epic of Baal, and on the sarcophagus of King Ahiram of Byblos, warning away tomb-robbers. In other words, this single curse is present in four different languages and in five different sorts of settings. Assuming that we might find the same thing to be true if we had fuller evidence about other curses, is there any reason for singling out the covenant or treaty as what was in the prophets' minds when they used such imagery? I would say, yes, not because of the verbal parallels and the parallels in imagery in themselves, but because there is such a similarity in function. These threats are meant to work in the same way in the treaties, or biblical covenant-reports, and in the prophets. The same conceptual framework appears in each, but the prophets appear at a later stage, after the treaty is already broken. It is not just that a treaty says the gods will send wild animals and that the prophets say that Yahweh will do so, but that in the treaty the curse is invoked as the consequence for rebellion and that the prophetic doom is announced for the same reason—as the consequence of rebellion. The significant thing is that Jeremiah says "There-fore a lion from the forest shall smite them." We need an adequate explanation for this "therefore." What framework is there that makes the coming of predators the just and normal outcome of the people's sin? There seems no escape from seeing the treaty relation in a special way as the foun-dation for this "therefore." Only if we presuppose a relation binding Israel to God on pain of curses do the prophets seem logical.

As it happens, we possess a remarkably clear instance outside the Bible, in the annals of the seventh-century As-syrian king Ashurbanipal, of the same sort of thinking in treaties. Before quoting this passage, however, we need to note that an earlier treaty, Sefire I, numbers among its curses an elaborate one threatening man and animals with dry breasts. "Should seven nur[ses] anoint [their breasts and] nurse a young boy, may he not have his fill; and should seven mares suckle a colt, may it not be sa[ted; and should seven] cows give suck to a calf, may it not have its fill; and should seven ewes suckle a lamb, [may it not be sa]ted." Ashurbanipal's annals tell how the Arabians under Uate' broke a treaty with their Assyrian suzerain. The vengeance of Ashurbanipal and the Assyrian gods was swift: the king beat the Arabians in battle and the god of pestilence raged among them. Famine struck them and they ate the flesh of their children. The gods "inflicted quickly upon them (all) the curses written down in their treaties. Even when the camel foals, the donkey foals, calves, or lambs would suckle seven times on their dams, they could not satisfy their stomachs with milk." [8] The Assyrian annalist has cast his description of the Arabians' distress in terms derived

8. The translation is that of A. Leo Oppenheim, in *Ancient Near Eastern Texts Relating to the Old Testament*, ed. James Pritchard, 2d ed. (Princeton, 1955), p. 300.

from the treaty they had broken. This is not only because of his preference for conventional expression—typical of these ancient writers—but also because of his conviction that a treaty by the gods would be enforced by the gods on the terms stated.

The above illustrates what I believe to have been true of the Israelite prophets. In the face of Israel's apostasy they declare Yahweh's judgment by drawing on curses traditionally associated with the covenant. If so, we have another large body of evidence that the prophets—and their hearers—thought in categories derived from the covenant and expressed themselves in language drawn from it.

This is important for our assessment of the prophets, who in anyone's view are some of the most interesting figures in the Old Testament. Much of modern scholarly study of the prophets has been devoted to prophetic psychology and attempts to describe and parallel the abnormal states of mind in which the prophets received their communications from God. Critical orthodoxy saw in the prophets the great creative figures in Israelite religion, the ones who made of a simple, natural faith a genuine monotheism vitally concerned with righteous living. Others more recently have tried to find the prophets a base in Israel's cult, in her organized institutions of worship. Though the present chapter is obviously not a full investigation of the role of the prophets, it may be enough to suggest modifications in all the above conceptions of the prophets' place in Israel's religion. Though we do have evidence, inside the Bible and out, that some prophets cultivated a kind of ecstasy and in this fit delivered their oracles, such prophetic rapture appears more and more to have been an incidental and extraneous feature of the profession, and one not especially characteristic of the literary prophets of Israel. Instead, they appear as rather sober figures who framed oracles that drew on a conventional stock of ideas and phrases with roots deep in Israel's history rather than in their own consciousness or individual genius. For this reason also we must reassess the once common idea of the prophets as innovators. Without in any way denying their creativity, it would seem from their use of Israel's most ancient religious heritage that they were in great part creative as religious reformers are. As for their role in Israelite society, the evidence of their deep attachment to covenant traditions would cast doubt on their supposed role in Israel's cult. There is really nothing at all in the covenant framework about sacrifice, and the literary prophets, on the whole, were so negative in their assessment of its religious worth that they would have been very disturbing fellows to have present at the shrine. But we do find the prophets at the court of the king, interfering in every possible way in the political life of their own land and on occasion lending a hand to a revolution in a foreign land. In most periods they enjoy great freedom to do so, and they castigate kings both for their personal lives and for their public policies. This kind of action is difficult to explain unless we see in them the bearers of a tradition older than the monarchy, the tradition of a day when Yahweh was king and prophets made known his will to the people. There is a persistent tradition in the Old Testament that Moses was a prophet. When this tradition may have arisen is hard to say, and it seems unlikely that Moses described himself in that fashion. But even if the tradition is late, it shows that Israelites recognized a similarity between the role of Moses, the mediator of the covenant, and the later prophets. This role was so firmly fixed within the religious consciousness of the people that the king had to give some hearing to the "prophet like unto Moses."

Why then, coming back to an old question, are the prophets so sparing of the word "covenant"? Here we must recall, as Mendenhall suggests, that the word "covenant" had been appropriated for the pact between Yahweh and the king, the rival covenant tradition. Although this is only a hypothesis, it seems to account best for the indirectness of prophetic references to a covenant with God. The mere word had, perhaps, been spoiled by its application to God's oath to the reigning monarch. To put it in a different and more general way, the covenant was no longer the practical constitution of Israel. Practically speaking, Israel was now a monarchy whose king was divinely chosen and whose temple was at the same time a royal chapel. By the time of the prophets, the theocratic ideal had passed from being what shaped the actual conduct of Israel's national life into the realm of religious ideas. By then it was truly a "biblical idea," and the prophets used the old idea mostly to announce the inevitable approach of judgment.

CHAPTER SEVEN

THE OLD AGE OF AN IDEA

As we approach the end of the story of covenant in the Old Testament, some characteristic symptoms of senescence appear. We encounter a vehement, almost desperate appeal for return to the old beliefs and the old ways, a repristination movement whose platform we know as the book of Deuteronomy. At this point, too, that is, toward the end of the Old Testament period, we find the most careful discrimination and intellectual synthesis of various covenant ideas in the calmly retrospective work we know as "P," the Priestly document of the Pentateuch. And finally, a telling sign that the idea and the society it had shaped were dying, we hear a prediction of an ideal covenant to come in an indistinct future, the vision of a prophet who could only hope that the covenant would be born again. This prophecy of a new covenant, the third of the late works with which the present chapter will be concerned, is that of the prophet Jeremiah.

The fifth book of Moses has a particularly unhappy title. Not only is "Deuteronomy" an inexact rendering of a phrase from the book, but the name is ugly and suggests something as dull as Leviticus. A better conception of the nature of the book may be gained from seeing how it affected King Josiah: "When the king heard the words of the book of the law, he tore his garments. And the king commanded . . . 'Go inquire of Yahweh for me and for the people and for all Judah concerning the words of this book that has been found, for great is the wrath of Yahweh which has been kindled against us.'" The impassioned sentences of Deuteronomy helped propel the most stringent reform ever attempted in Judah's history and will serve us as a measure of the continuing vitality of the covenant idea, of the changes in its conception, and of the heroic efforts necessary to put the covenant back in force as a social reality. Before turning to the book itself, however, we need to consider the ceremony by which it was adopted as the platform for Josiah's reform.

"There had never been one like him—a king who turned to Yahweh with all his heart and all his soul and all his strength, according to the whole law of Moses, and after him there never arose another like him." This lavish praise is for Josiah of Judah (about 640–609 B.C.), and he earned it. Even so, we may observe that almost anything would have looked good after the long apostasy under Manasseh, Josiah's grandfather. Although it is true that a certain amount of homage to Assyrian gods was forced on Manasseh, given his country's position as a pitifully weak client of Assyria, Manasseh seems to have had a positive relish for whatever was debased, obscene, and superstitious in foreign religion. Josiah, who was only eight when he came to the throne, and eighteen when he began repairs on the temple, was no doubt swept along by popular revulsion at the low condition to which the people of Yahweh had fallen. Then, too, his religious reform was twined with a resurgent nationalism, for Assyria was approaching its death throes and her influence in Palestine grew steadily weaker as Josiah's reign advanced. The old religious tradition was of an Israel made up of twelve tribes and of a kingdom granted to David stretching far beyond the confines of little Judah. With Assyria's threat diminishing, it was not wholly unreasonable for Josiah to dream of regaining the territory of the "lost ten tribes," especially since some descendants of these tribes were not lost at all but lived in their former home and maintained a kind of worship of Yahweh. So we must think of a sincerely pious young king, under the influence of Yahwistic priests and the pressure of revival in the air, suddenly confronted with a book bearing the prestigious name of Moses, which denounced in detail and with the most appalling curses the religion actually practiced in Judah.

> Then the king sent word around, and all the elders of Judah and Jerusalem gathered to him. And the king went up to the house of Yahweh, accompanied by all the men of Judah and all the inhabitants of Jerusalem, with the priests and the prophets and all the people from least to greatest, and he read in their hearing all the words of the book of the covenant which had been found in the house of Yahweh. The king stood by a pillar and made a covenant before Yahweh, to walk after Yahweh and to keep his commandments and ordinances and statutes, with all his heart and all his soul, to establish all the words of this covenant that were written in this book. And all the people entered into the covenant (II Kings 23:1–3).

Following this impressive ceremony, the king and his people make good their vow and carry out their promise with a rigor and attention to detail which has convinced scholars that the book they were following was much the same as our Deuteronomy.

Knowing how fundamental was the practice of covenant-making both in religious tradition and everyday life, we are not surprised to find a covenant turning up at this crisis in Judah's religious life, nor to discover that in some respects it is like the covenants made in the earliest days. It involves obedience to norms established by Yahweh, and there is a written document in connection with it, the familiar "text of the covenant." The form of words for the king's action is familiar: literally, "he cut a covenant"; and the idea that one man acts for the people is also familiar from the examples of Moses and Joshua. We will shortly look at the book of Deuteronomy itself and see that it contains a great many ancient terms and patterns of thought connected with treaty-making.

Yet for all this, the action as a whole is different in intention and form. Yahweh is not involved in the same way. In the Israelites' view of the Sinai pact, he is the initiator and the major partner. He addresses Israel directly, and the form of address is "I" and "you." Here the covenant is "before Yahweh." It is entirely the idea of the king and the people. Although it is implied that Yahweh will hold them to this promise, that is only what he would require in the case of any promise made on oath and does not make him a partner to the agreement. This is a unilateral promise and does not specify or imply any role for Yahweh to perform beyond that of the recipient of the promise. To emphasize a related but different aspect of contrast, no new relation is brought into being. At Sinai, Israel and Yahweh were for the first time bound to one another, and in subsequent covenants, new groups entered into relation with this new god and at the same time into new relation with one another. In Josiah's covenant there is no question of Yahweh's acting to make this gathering his people or of the people accepting him as their god, for that had all been settled long ago. The aim is rather that of pledging allegiance to a body of laws and of defining obedience to Yahweh as obedience to this corpus. Coming after a time when Manasseh's abominations had dominated, there was a need for new regulations to bring Israel's life into conformity with her ancient faith. It seemed especially good to centralize sacrificial worship at one place, the better to keep it pure of paganism. But since the king never had power to make new laws (though he could levy taxes), the only recognized way of asserting the common determination to abide by a new standard was through some sort of covenant.[1] Note, too, that here history plays no role. This may be accidental, since we cannot assume that the account in Kings supplies every detail connected with the event, yet perhaps it is not simple chance. The stress in covenant history is consistently on the gracious acts of Yahweh, leading up to and motivating obedience to the pact. In this context the focus is very much on earth, on the acts good or bad of the kings of Judah, and the covenant entered into is more a matter of human resolution than an offer of God as the last of a series of saving acts. In sum, this sort of promissory covenant was a revival of older covenant ideas, but like any revival, it was not the same as the original thing.

Note especially the sequel. Josiah sets earnestly and energetically to work and enforces the Deuteronomic regulations with all the force his kingdom could command. This too is different from the days when "every man did what was right in his own eyes." It would, of course, be wrong to say that the old covenant did not involve some norms for fellowship with Yahweh. On the contrary, that was always a main feature of the covenant. But in the days of the judges there was no centralized state to enforce in a uniform way a detailed code of positive prescriptions. Each village community and each tribal group had freedom, under the covenant, to regulate its own affairs, and the covenant did not have the effect of putting more power in the hands of some ruler or group of rulers. Now, in Josiah's day, the conclusion of a covenant of king and people lends the backing of religion to the actions of the secular arm, and the list

1. The discussion of the covenant under Josiah presented here is indebted principally to the account given by George Mendenhall in his article on "Covenant" in *The Interpreter's Dictionary of the Bible* (New York and Nashville, 1962), vol. I.

of stipulations is not a simple Ten Commandments but the detailed regulations of a developed body of laws.

This prepares the way for the form which religious covenants took after the Babylonian exile, under Ezra and Nehemiah, and since these pacts resemble so closely that made under King Josiah, we may consider them briefly before going on with Deuteronomy. The first covenant under Ezra, described in Ezra 9 and 10, was a sworn agreement on the part of the returned exiles that all those who had married foreign women should divorce them, a decision that affected a great many. The scene is memorable; Ezra, utterly inflexible, with all the force of the law of Moses behind him, confronts the assembled men of Judah, "shivering because of this matter, and because of the heavy rain." This use of a sworn agreement is not new; it is covenant for the sake of revival, as under Josiah. The same holds for the more elaborate agreement described in Nehemiah 9 and 10. Critical problems abound here[2] but do not substantially affect our assessment of the sort of covenant involved. Familiar themes reappear. Chapter 9 gives the history of God's dealings with Israel, beginning with Abram and continuing through the monarchy to their present misery. "Behold, we are slaves today, in the land which you gave our fathers, to eat of its fruit and its goodness, we are slaves." "Because of all this" they make a pact, described in the succeeding chapter (if these two originally belong together) as "a curse and an oath," the stipulations being that they would "walk in the law of God, given through Moses, the servant of God, to observe and do all the commandments of Yahweh our Lord, his laws and ordinances." As a closing feature, certain

2. The problems involved are treated lucidly and concisely in the new commentary on Ezra and Nehemiah by Jacob M. Myers in The Anchor Bible, vol. 14 (Garden City, N. Y., 1965), especially pp. 158–80.

specific regulations are singled out for special mention, including the payment of a tax for support of the temple. In essentials, the pattern is familiar. The covenant has become an affirmation of loyalty to a code of conduct, a pledge of allegiance serving the cause of religious reform.

Returning now to Deuteronomy, we may well ponder an obvious feature of the book: its length. Deuteronomy is longer than any covenant text known to us, even if one discounts certain parts of the book as later additions, as most do, if only because it is hard to believe that the high priest could have read all thirty-four chapters to Josiah at one sitting, or that the king in turn would have read all this to the people. So most scholars believe that Josiah's law book did not contain absolutely all the present components of the work, and they divide the book at some obvious seams, such as the poems of Moses which form several of the final chapters. Even with these omissions, however, Deuteronomy is long. And the style underlines this characteristic. It is the opposite of terse. The writer never uses one word where he can think of two, and he always can. It is not: "These are the commandments," but over and over "These are the commandments, the statutes, and the judgments." This is not to say that the style is unimpressive. The writer achieves a vehemence, a volume, one might say, which is well suited for reproducing the thunders of Yahweh's great indignation. But the length and the fulsome style are important for the history of the covenant idea. They mark Deuteronomy as a late state in the development of the notion. Symphonies grow longer, orchestras grow bigger, not only because composers need to express new musical ideas, but in the end out of a hope that more brass will render thin ideas more impressive. Deuteronomy is a Symphony of a Thousand, which brings us covenant ideas of very high antiquity, some of them in a fulness not found elsewhere—but at the same time the bombastic quality in the work suggests that the ideas themselves had lost some of their power to convince.

Although language and style put the present form of Deuteronomy into the seventh century B.C., scholars for the most part no longer think that the book was forged to suit the reform of Josiah. It was inevitable that this hypothesis should be suggested, once critics had shown how well the provisions of the book fit what Josiah did, but now that several generations have had time to think about it, it appears that the fit is not exact—Levites are not treated in the same way in the book and in Josiah's practice—and recent research has discovered evidence that ties the ultimate origin of Deuteronomy to the northern kingdom. It is plausible to suppose that an earlier form of the book, or at least the traditions on which it is based, was brought to the south by refugees after the fall of Samaria, the northern capital, in 722, and it may well have experienced the fate described in the Bible: left to moulder in the temple under Manasseh and Amon, it came to light only with Josiah.

The size of the book makes it hard to see its framework on a first reading, but once this outline is extracted, any reader can at once detect the impress of the covenant form.

Moses' first discourse—the history of God's dealing with Israel, 1:1–4:43
Moses' second discourse, 4:44–28:69
 Introduction, 4:44–49
 Covenant and Commandments
  The Ten Commandments, 5:1–33
  Exhortation to keep them for the sake of God's grace in history, and of future blessings and curses, 6:1–11:32
  The Laws, 12:1–26:19
A covenant ceremony at Shechem, 27:1–26
Blessings and curses, 28:1–69

There are several more chapters, most likely later additions though showing marks of the same style here and there, but these 28 are enough for our purpose. The elements found here reproduce much of the outline of the Sinai covenant, or of the Hittite suzerainty treaty: history first, then stipulations, then blessings and curses. Chapter 27, with its proleptic account of a ceremony carried on at Shechem, or rather, at the two mountains that flank it, Ebal and Gerizim, seems intrusive as far as this book is concerned; but with its details on how a ritual of blessing and cursing was to be carried on, it is both ancient and thoroughly within the covenant pattern. Thus the structure as a whole makes Deuteronomy "the biblical document of the covenant *par excellence*," as W. L. Moran has styled it.

Even more impressive than this structural resemblance, however, is the amount of detailed correspondence between the language and thought of Deuteronomy and that of extrabiblical treaties. This relatively late biblical book transmits words and concepts that go back, in many cases, to the second millennium b.c. A characteristic designation for Israel in Deuteronomy is 'am segullah, a combination hard to translate literally, approximately "people who are the private property" (of Yahweh), "peculiar people" in the Authorized Version. This rather rare Hebrew word has turned up in a Ugaritic letter, where it is used by the Hittite suzerain, evidently to describe the king of Ugarit as his "private property," though the context is somewhat broken so that one cannot be certain. As Moran has pointed out, Deuteronomy avoids the term "whore after" other gods, much used elsewhere in Scripture, and prefers the phrase "to walk after" a god, in the sense "to serve, worship" a god.[3] This

3. Moran's views, on which this discussion relies, are presented in his "The Ancient Near Eastern Background of the Love of God in Deuteronomy," *Catholic Biblical Quarterly*, 25 (1963): 77–87. I have used Moran's translation of the Akkadian passages quoted.

fits the usage of the El Amarna letters, which speak of serving a superior king with the same idiom. "With all your heart" has become such a cliché in modern speech that we may miss the biblical origin of the phrase, to say nothing of sensing that it is especially characteristic of Deuteronomic style. But this is another mark, as Moran has pointed out, of Deuteronomy's saturation with treaty language. The stipulation found repeatedly in the treaties is that the vassal must fight for his lord "with all his heart."

The love of God is another peculiar stress of Deuteronomy, and a still more remarkable instance of the book's conservation of very old covenant ideas. "Love" has been used in such a variety of ways in western history that considerable scholarly effort has been devoted to discriminating the various species of affection to which the term has been applied. Deuteronomy's brand of love is an especially interesting one for two reasons: it represents a type of love very different from most recent conceptions, and it is the mother lode of much other influential biblical teaching about love for God. "Love" in Deuteronomy can be commanded: "You shall love Yahweh your God with all your heart, and with all your soul, and with all your might" (6:5). This means living in a relation of worship and service to the deity. "You shall love Yahweh your god, and keep his observances, his statutes, his laws, and his commandments for all time" (11:1). The whole commandment can be summed up thus: ". . . to love Yahweh, your God, to walk in all his ways, and to cleave to him" (11:22). "To love Yahweh" is linked inseparably with "to serve Him" (11:13). "Know that Yahweh your God is the one God, the faithful God, who keeps covenant and faith with those who love him and keep his commandments for a thousand generations" (7:9). We have heard these words so often that their doctrine does not seem surprising, but we need to remember that one theory of love, of very potent influence, has held that duty and love are incompatible. Here they are nearly identified.

It is W. L. Moran who has identified the language of treaties and covenants as the profane source for this conception of the love of God. Though there may be earlier examples, the first common use of "love" in the language of diplomacy is found in the archives of El Amarna. The relation that exists between "brothers," that is, equal partners in a treaty, is "love": "May my brother preserve love toward me ten times more than did his father, and we will go on loving my brother fervently" (29:166). This love is not only the proper feeling between equal partners, however, but is the way that Pharaoh regards his vassals. "If the king my lord loves his faithful servant let him send back the three men!" (123:23). And above all, it is the way vassals are to consider their lord. To love is equal to being a servant. "My lord, just as I love the king my lord, so (do) the king of Nuhasse, the king of Ni'i . . . —all these kings are servants of my lord" (53:40–44). Rib-Addi of Byblos uses "love" to describe the divided loyalties of his rebellious city: "Behold the city! Half of it loves the sons of Abdi-ashirta and half of it loves my lord." This kind of language survives into the first millennium, where we find it in the vassal-treaties of king Esarhaddon of Assyria. Note that love is here commanded as a duty toward the suzerain. "You will love Ashurbanipal as yourselves." And also in the Bible, "love" is used in nonreligious contexts for the attitude of treaty partners. When David died, "Hiram king of Tyre sent his servants to Solomon because he had heard that he had been anointed king in place of his father, for Hiram loved David always" (I Kings 5:15). Hiram follows perfectly correct procedure, since treaties needed to be renewed on the death of one partner, and the exchange of embassies brings about a covenant with Solomon. Thus "Hiram always loved David" might be restated "Hiram had always been a true ally of David's." Love here is in part the language of emotion, in part the language of international law.

Thus the treaty relation also provides the source for the principal biblical concept of the love man owes to God, a love consisting of fidelity and obedience. The presentation here has perhaps stressed too much the legal source of the idea and the obligatory character of this love. "Love your lord" is not, however, even in treaties, simply a polite way of saying "Obey or else"; it is not merely a synonym for obedience. The ancient kings at least made an effort to put their relations to vassals on some other level than that of naked power and forced obedience. "Love your lord," like much of the rest of this terminology, words like "brother, father, with your whole heart," expresses a desire, no doubt rather naïve, to effect sincere affection and heartfelt loyalty as bonds of peace. To say then that "Love the Lord your god" is ultimately legal language is not to take it out of the realm of emotion but only to say that the legal concept shapes the emotional term. To love is to set one's sincere affections on the covenant Lord and to give this affection its expression in loyal service.

But if we find this ancient covenant idea, love of God, expressed more clearly in Deuteronomy than in any other Old Testament book, we also find in its ideas and language evidences that the book is late. Deuteronomy is a revival of covenant ideas, bringing some ideas in relatively pristine form, but changing and combining others. This is the case in the book's attitude toward the covenant with the fathers, and with the king. As we have seen, the covenant of obedience binding Israel, and the covenant of promise binding Yahweh, were originally two separate things, not at all easy to reconcile with one another. In Deuteronomy, however, they are combined in classic fashion, so that even if the tension is not resolved, some of the essential features of both are preserved. The oath God swore to Abraham is, of course, prior. It is the unchanging guarantee that Yahweh is committed to them. This is then meshed with the Sinai covenant theme as part of the history. "It was not because you outnumbered any other people that Yahweh desired you and chose you, for you were the least of all peoples, but because Yahweh loved you, and kept the oath which he swore to your fathers that he brought you out with a strong hand and redeemed you from the house of bondage, from the power of Pharaoh, king of Egypt" (7:7–8). And since the prior oath of God is thus one of his gracious acts toward Israel, it is one thing that should motivate their humble obedience. The quotation above is preceded and followed by vigorous exhortations to obey. Remember that Deuteronomy was published after a discouraging period of servitude to Assyria and at a time when fresh hope for the nation was beginning to stir. The Sinai covenant offered little grounds for optimism, but some hope could be garnered from the promise to Abraham. "When you are in distress and all these things have overtaken you, in the latter time, then you will return to Yahweh your god and hearken to his voice, for Yahweh your god is a merciful god who will not let you down or destroy you, and who will not forget the covenant with your fathers, that which he swore to them" (4:31).

Deuteronomy's treatment of the monarchy is interesting. Coming at a time when David's sons had occupied the throne for about three hundred years, it would have been either utopian or revolutionary for Deuteronomy to picture an Israel without a king. Instead, the king must somehow be fitted into the theological scheme. So the writer has Moses foresee a situation in which the people might want to set a king over them, and he provides a little guide for future princes.

When you come to the land which Yahweh your God
will give you, and take it over and inhabit it, should you say,
"I want to set over me a king like all other nations around me,"
then be sure to set over you that king whom Yahweh your
God shall choose. You must set over you one of your brethren;
you cannot set over you a foreigner, one who is not of your
brethren. Only he must not acquire many horses, and send
people back down to Egypt to get more horses, when Yahweh
has said to you "You shall not go back on this way again."
Nor should he acquire many wives, so that his heart be not
led astray, nor should he acquire much gold or silver. And
when he takes the throne to rule, he shall get for himself a
written copy of this law, on a scroll, from the Levitical priests,
and keep it by him all the days of his life, that he may learn
to fear Yahweh his God, and keep and do all the words of this
law, and the statutes, so that he may not think himself better
than others, or turn aside to right or left from the commandment, that his reign in Israel, and that of his sons, may endure long (Deuteronomy 17:14–20).

There is in this a grudging recognition of the dynastic
principle—"and his sons" is the evidence—and even of the
divine election of the king, for he must be "that king whom
Yahweh your God shall choose." Even so, the king occupies
a rather humble position, and a decidedly ambiguous one.
Even if his is a sacred role he is reminded that it is one
found in all the nations, not a distinctively originally Israelite institution. And even if he is chosen by Yahweh, the
covenant that applies to him is "this law." That is, he is
subject to the Deuteronomic restatement of the Mosaic
covenant, not the blessed recipient of a splendid guarantee
of peace, prosperity, and the eternal continuance of his line.
We may doubt that the pietistic ideal of a king who reads
his Deuteronomy faithfully throughout life was very often
realized. Even so we must recall that a vigorous king, Josiah,
accepted this book as the divine law and thus expressed his
willingness to have his reign described as a monarchy definitely limited by a prior contract between God and the
people. In the end this ideal prevails, to such an extent that

the Jews after the exile are able to dispense with the king altogether, as their state takes the shape of a community subject to a written divine law whose authoritative interpreters are the priests.

The close parallel between one of the curses in Deuteronomy and a passage in Esarhaddon's vassal treaties has been commented on in the preceding chapter. It seems extremely unlikely that sheer coincidence can account for the occurrence of a malediction involving copper heavens and an earth turned to iron, in the seventh-century Assyrian treaty, in Leviticus, and in Deuteronomy. I do not believe that we need go as far as some scholars have and speculate that perhaps this curse occurred in a treaty between Assyria and Judah, whence the biblical writers learned it. On the other hand, it is correct to say that the three texts with this curse are drawing on a common literary or legal tradition and that this tradition was not very old. None of our earlier treaties contain such a curse; it is not a traditional curse in other kinds of texts; and the mention of iron makes it unlikely that it was framed much before the Iron Age! If this judgment is correct, a point of some importance is established: Israelite thought about the covenant with God remained open to influences from the language of profane treaty-making throughout Israel's history. It is not that a legal form supplied the basic analogy at the beginning of her religious history and that this then developed independently, cut off from any secular influence; rather, Israel's theologians remained aware that their pact with God was a treaty, much like a treaty between men, so that as the profane practice underwent change and development it was likely to modify her religious thought in some way. This view is confirmed by the length of the section of curses in Deuteronomy. The writer's imagination, and his erudition, exhaust themselves in predicting the evils to come on an unfaithful people.

This is not the fashion in the treaties closest to the time of Moses, but there is a lengthening of the section of curses through the ages, the climax coming in the treaties closest in time to Deuteronomy, the vassal treaties of Esarhaddon, which have over 250 lines of curses. Thus Deuteronomy shows both the internal development of covenant theology in Israel and the continued influence of secular and foreign forms.

Like "Deuteronomy," the unlovely designation "P," or even the fuller title "The Priestly Document," gives no very clear indication of the content of the Pentateuchal source to which it is attached. It is true that the document so labelled contains much material written by priests for priests, details of sanctuary furnishings and the niceties of ancient rituals of such a monumental dullness as to test severely the endurance of the most dedicated Bible-reader. But "P" also has given us the framework for the Pentateuch, which is to say the outline of world history accepted without challenge in all Christendom until not so long ago. Now, if the "P" version's ordering of the generations since creation has been so enormously influential, it would be unjust to conclude that this was due only to the credulity of a prescientific, Bible-dominated age. It is fairer to give recognition to the merits of this anonymous work, to acknowledge the fundamental reasonableness of its account of creation (Genesis 1), to concede the plausibility of the way it divides the ages and nations of the world, and even to pay credit to the soberness and austerity of the style, for the very dryness of the chain of begats lends credibility to the narrative. In "P," then, we have to do with a writer, or more probably, a school of writers, who have reflected long on what they have to say and who practice great economy in saying it.

An important part of the "P" articulation of history is a sequence of covenants with God. In most cases, a new age begins with a new pact, for "P" is not telling a secular history but a story of God's successive dealings with men. No covenant is mentioned at the very beginning, but after the deluge God concludes a covenant (berit) with Noah, marking a new stage in human history and in the "P" version of it. The covenant is one of pure grace, as was shown in detail in an earlier chapter. God commits himself to preserve from then on the orderly succession of seasons, and no catastrophic flood will come again. "P" then treats the descendants of Noah until Abraham, at which time a narrowing takes place, and the interest then focuses only on the patriarchs, the immediate ancestors of Israel. This turning point has its berit also, a covenant of promise, binding God without corresponding obligation on the human partner. Note that "P" still does not use the name "Yahweh," at this point, and also that in his scheme of things there is no sacrifice to God through this whole time. God has only begun his saving work, and the whole apparatus of sacred action connected with the sacrificial cult waits for a new dispensation.

God's full and final ordering of things comes with Moses and Sinai, and again there is a covenant. Or is there? If it seems hard to think of a writer telling about Sinai without mentioning a covenant, we need to realize that this is just what "P" seems to have done, at least in the view of many scholars. The word "P" uses for "covenant" when speaking of Noah and Abraham (and Phineas, the hero of the Baal Peor incident, Numbers 25), berit, is never used for the ordinances dispensed at Sinai or for the institutions and apparatus connected with Sinai. Thus where the other Pentateuchal sources speak of the "ark of the covenant" (berit), the Priestly writer never does, preferring a different Hebrew term. If the Priestly document does not regard Sinai as involving a covenant, then it is at this point strikingly different from the other Pentateuchal sources, and scholars have assessed the significance of this difference in various ways. The most arresting analysis finds that "P" is a writer who knows only of a covenant of grace, of a divine gospel but no law, like an Old Testament Paul! The argument by which this view is advanced is logical, but it reaches so unexpected a conclusion that the premises need to be reconsidered. Who would ever have dreamed of finding the Apostle bracketed with a writer who numbers among his principle interests chronology, genealogy, and ritual?

The key to a correct understanding of the "P" covenant theology lies in the word used for the Sinai pact, ʿeduth. Because it contains the Hebrew consonants ʿayin and daleth, this noun has traditionally been connected by translators, beginning with the Septuagint, to a verb containing the same consonants and meaning "to testify." The "P" terminology has commonly been translated "the tablets of the testimony," "ark of the testimony," and so on, and although the exact meaning of such phrases is not immediately apparent, they convey no suggestion of a pact. It seems that this sort of translation, in spite of its antiquity, is wide of the mark and that ʿeduth is actually another name for "covenant." Thus the new Jewish Publication Society version of the Torah (1962) renders it "pact," which is convenient because it is accurate and at the same time preserves in English a distinction between the two Hebrew terms. The reader may be slightly mystified at how such a shift in translation of a fairly common Hebrew term is justified; he may suspect that semitists are availing themselves of Humpty Dumpty's principle for the treatment of words. That is not so in the present case (though it does happen). The necessity of redefining ʿeduth was demonstrated in 1955 by William F. Albright, on the basis of a re-examination of the usage of the word in the Bible and on evidence from other Semitic languages, especially the Aramaic ꜥdy(ꜣ) (exact vowels are unknown), which occurs in the Sefire treaties in contexts such as the following: "The treaty (ꜥdy) of Bir-Gaꜣyah, king of KTK, with Matiꜥel . . . ."[4] I shall omit further details, for the sake of those readers who feel that they have already been told more of Hebrew lexical problems than they care to know. It seemed permissible to indulge in this much philology, however, as a reminder that, although there is more glamor to digging pots out of the ground than in digging new meanings out of texts, archaeologists have done no more for biblical studies than those who grind at grammar. Under ordinary circumstances, to recast the old saying, one word is worth ten thousand sherds. A more practical reason for the above discussion of Hebrew ꜥeduth is that we must have this term in mind in order to understand the Priestly writer's peculiar method of fitting covenant together with other concepts that are important to him.

In some ways, the "P" treatment of the Sinai pact is not at all peculiar to our way of thinking, but rather anticipates the discrimination between various sorts of covenants which has been carried out again in modern times. He has two terms. *Berit*, "covenant," he uses only for God's promises, those oaths that bind God only. *ꜣEduth*, "pact," he uses only for what was concluded at Sinai. Since this

4. Professor Albright presented his views on Hebrew ꜥeduth and related terms in a paper, still unpublished, delivered at the 1955 meeting of the Society of Biblical Literature. I am indebted to Professor Albright for putting at my disposal his notes on the subject, which have been augmented since 1955 by his own further researches and the contributions of others. My account of the various covenants in the Priestly document was presented before the Society of Biblical Literature in 1965. An extended study, combining Professor Albright's observations and my own, is in preparation.

term, elsewhere in the Bible, is closely associated, and practically synonymous, with words for "ordinance, law," it seems reasonable to say that "P" meant to make the point that the Sinai pact was different from the others in that it laid the yoke of obligation on Israel. As stated above, the Priestly writer was a precise theologian, and this drawing of nice distinctions between different covenants is quite in keeping with the general character of his work.

There is nothing in this to strike us as eccentric, and except for its greater precision, the "P" account of what happened at Sinai is much like the other Pentateuchal sources. Yet the Priestly writer does seem peculiar in other respects, both in his emphases and his mode of procedure. His individual conception of the covenant arises from a desire to stress and justify Israel's cult. "P" set out to describe the details of how the tent sanctuary was constructed and furnished, how the priests were ordained, and how they were to go about their rituals. But he faced a problem. What does all this ritual apparatus and rubrics have to do with the covenant, with the pact made at Sinai which he regarded as a climactic point in world history? If we are correct in thinking that the international suzerainty treaty was the ultimate model for the Sinai covenant, then we can readily see that this sort of agreement has next to nothing to do with cult. Treaties make contact with the cultic sphere only in the ritual surrounding the swearing and in deposit of the copies in temples, but these are peripheral matters. As this treaty was adapted by Israel for the pact between God and men, it seems to have been directed almost exclusively toward social obligations rather than ritual. Israel must not worship other gods, but the commandment says nothing about how she should worship hers. This does not mean that earliest Israel did not sacrifice to Yahweh, have ordained priests, shrines, and so on, but it does mean that this formal worship had no necessary connection to the covenant. Just as the covenant left most areas of Israelite life open for the preservation of old custom or the introduction of new forms, so ritual seems to have been from the point of view of the covenant an adiaphoron, a matter of indifference. The Priestly writer, like many biblical theologians of our own time, felt a need to give some account of how these two separate spheres are joined.

He does this in part through puns. We probably do not expect to meet the lowest form of humor in the most serious theological exposition, but in this modern taste is different from that of the ancient Israelites. The very sound of a word, its resemblance to another one, was felt to be significant, even if the likeness was very superficial. Naming went on the principle *nomen est omen*—a man's name is an augury of his fate. At the climax of his Song of the Vineyard (5:1–7), which is not only serious but even savage in its tone, the prophet Isaiah uses a double play on words, and this is not meant or felt to be a lapse into humor. Thus if "P" puns, it is done with serious intent, and at least ancient hearers would have been impressed by the list of sound-alikes that he is able to pile up. The central purpose of ritual, in his view, is that of *meeting* with God, expressed in various related Hebrew words: no'ad (verbal form), "to meet, encounter"; mo'ed (nominal form), "meeting, appointed time"; and another nominal form 'edah, "congregation." Israel is an 'edah, a "congregation," and the tent-shrine is the "tent of meeting" (mo'ed). There Yahweh "meets" (no'ad) with the Israelites. Speaking of the use of the sacred trumpets, "P" uses all three, "And when they blow them, all the congregation ['edah] shall assemble [no'edu] before you at the entrance to the tent of meeting [mo'ed]" (Numbers 10:3). From this solid pier of terminology "P" erects a bridge to the covenant idea. 'eduth, his word for the Sinai pact, with its combination of the consonants ' and d ('ayin and daleth), sounds a lot like his "meeting" words, as though they were all derived from the same base. This is not so, this being the kind of etymology in which the vowels count for nothing at all and the consonants for very little, but it permits a barrage of assonance that leaves the impression that "covenant" and "meeting" really are much the same. So the tabernacle is interchangeably "tent of 'edut" and "tent of mo'ed," and "P" likes to combine the elements in sentences: "You shall put some of it [incense] in front of the pact ['edut] in the tent of meeting [mo'ed], where I will meet ['iwwa'ed] with you" (Exodus 30:36; compare 30:6; Numbers 17:19).

This theology through paronomasia is a bit bizarre, but another of the "P" devices for linking cultus and covenant seems less strained. He emphasizes the fact that the covenant, in its sacred box, is also the central object in the cult, around which the whole tabernacle and ultimately all Israel was arranged. Through this stress on the physical proximity of these two elements in Israel's religion he presumably meant to suggest an affinity between them at a spiritual level.

Scholars have noticed that the "P" account of God at Sinai is of a figure more distant than the deity pictured by "J" and "E." The covenant in "J" and "E" is an awesome thing, issued with all the majesty and fear-inspiring glory of Yahweh, and yet there is a certain mutuality in the story in Exodus 24:3–8 as the Israelites are carefully made aware of the contents of the pact by Moses and are given repeated opportunities to decide whether they will accept or reject it. Another old source reports a covenant meal at which some Israelite dignitaries "saw God, and ate and drank" (Exodus 24:11). In "P" God simply issues his commands to Moses atop the mountain and hands him the two tablets of the pact, "tablets of stone written by the finger of God" (Exodus

31:18). This is then enforced without asking for the assent of the people. In my opinion, the "P" account reflects the realities of Assyrian treaty-practice during the period of their domination, a time familiar to the author or authors of the Priestly document. "Now I am sending you herewith my personal official, Nabu-eriba, my third-man-on-the-chariot, Nergal-shar-usur, (and) Akkulanu, a temple-official of the god Aššur, with the tablet containing the treaty with me. The treaty is established." [5] Thus writes the king of Assyria to a subject. He is sending a dignitary with the treaty, which is in effect therewith. The irresistible power of the monarch is perfectly evident, and the diplomatic form makes no effort to conceal it. Even though the vassal would have had to go through a formal ceremony in a temple, there was no question of his refusing the treaty or deflecting the will of the sovereign. Just as Deuteronomy seems to reflect some later features borrowed from contemporary covenants, so "P" seems to be influenced at this point by a practice in which the making of a treaty was in fact the issuance of a unilateral decree by a sovereign power. If so, it fit his purpose well. There is really no way of showing how a particular ritual arises from the covenant with God necessarily or logically. Given Israel's concept of Yahweh as a just and merciful God, it follows that those in league with him must not murder, or steal, and so on, but there is no natural link between the character of Yahweh and the precept that the offering for the ordination of priests includes "the fat of the ram, the fat tail, the fat that covers the intestines, the protuberance on the liver, the kidneys and the fat over them and the right thigh" (Exodus 29:22). The justification for these ritual details is in consequence made

5. The translation of the Akkadian is that of *The Assyrian Dictionary*, vol. 1 (Chicago, 1964), entry for adû, except that I have given the proper names in full and substituted "treaty" for "adê-agreement."

to be divine fiat, and the whole "P" picture of the covenant transaction at Sinai enhances this picture of God as the remote, irresistible sovereign who issues his orders through an emissary.

The religion of Israel assigned an important place to history. This lent a wonderful concreteness to her credo: Yahweh was her God because at a particular time and place he had delivered her from Egypt. There is movement and life in the picture: once they were wandering Aramaeans, but then God took them; once they had no land, but Yahweh gave them this land. All the sacred institutions of Israel found their justification in some act of God in the past; the existence of the people rested on the pact with Abraham and the exodus, her possession of territory on God-given victories, her king descended from a king of God's choice, her holy city elected by God at David's time. But this meant that the passage of time and the chances of history could make questionable every precious tenet. Perhaps that exodus in the dim past was by now a mere migration, as meaningless as any other. Amos dared to say it: "Indeed, I brought Israel up out of the land of Egypt—and the Philistines from Caphtor, and Aram from Kir" (Amos 9:7). It was especially easy to question the continuing significance of the exodus when the Israelites found themselves, quite unexpectedly, in exile, in a different house of bondage. It was hard to maintain a lively faith in the election of David's house when the reigning king was an apostate tyrant, or when the monarch was himself a prisoner in Babylon; and hard to be a fundamentalist about the inviolability of Zion when the city was in ruins. So as the foundations of Israel's life eroded and crumbled, a process of reinterpretation began. If Israel is again in bondage, prophets say there will be a new exodus. With the decline of the ruling house prophets look for a new and different anointed of the Lord. With

Zion in ruins they dream plans for a new temple and a new Jerusalem. So too, in the midst of a book of comfort for the exiles of Israel and Judah, Jeremiah prophesies a new covenant (31:31–34):[6]

> Behold the days are coming, is the oracle of Yahweh, when I will make a new covenant with the house of Israel and the house of Judah, not like the covenant I made with their fathers when I took their hand and led them out of the land of Egypt. They broke that covenant with me, though I was their husband, is the oracle of Yahweh. Instead this is the covenant which I shall make with the house of Israel in time to come (oracle of Yahweh): I will put my law within them, and write it upon their hearts. I will be their God and they will be my people. No longer will each man have to teach his neighbor or brother, saying "Know Yahweh!" for all of them will know me, from the least of them to the greatest (oracle of Yahweh), for I will forgive their iniquity, and I will remember their sin no longer.

For Jeremiah, the old covenant is a thing of the past. He does not call for a return to it. Jeremiah had, after all, experienced the reform of Josiah, which was an attempt to rally the people around the old Mosaic standard, and as is plain from other words of his the result was a bitter disappointment. "They broke that covenant with me" dismisses the old order laconically but finally.

The new covenant, to be made in the indefinite future, the days to come, is, however, much like the old. It will

6. I have purposely omitted any discussion of the use of "covenant" (berit) in the work of the anonymous prophet called Second Isaiah (roughly Isaiah 40–55; the limits of the work are disputed), in spite of his use of the term in two important passages, 42:6 and 49:8. In my opinion, we do not yet understand what is meant by the key phrase berit ʿam, even at the linguistic level. For a discussion of the problem and possible solutions, the reader may consult Christopher R. North, The Second Isaiah (Oxford, 1964), p. 112. Walter Eichrodt, in his Theology of the Old Testament, trans. J. A. Baker (Philadelphia, 1961), 1:61–62, offers a suggestive account of what the passages in question might mean for the history of covenant.

come from Yahweh's initiative; it will not be a king's program of reform. And its contents can be summed up in the old formula: "I will be their God and they will be my people." The newness lies in the idea that the demands of the covenant will be written on their hearts. Each man will implicitly know Yahweh, that is, recognize him as Lord and not simply pay him the token of lip service which society expected. This state of affairs will come about because Yahweh will forgive their iniquity and forget their sin. The tradition was that any covenant was based on God's gracious act, and in Jeremiah's new covenant this fundamental place is supplied by Yahweh's forgiveness. This is visionary, as visionary as the peaceable kingdom, where the lion and lamb lie down together, or the desert that blossoms like the rose, or the river of life flowing out of the new Jerusalem. For Jeremiah, covenant has become a symbol and a hope. He does not expect to see it in his time, though we might say that he himself, as one born out of due time, experienced the forgiveness and knowledge of God which he foresaw.

CHAPTER EIGHT

ALL THINGS NEW

"A parhelion—a double sun—a secondary sun, that should shine for centuries with equal proofs for its own authenticity as existed for the original sun, would not be more shocking to the sense and to the auguries of man than a secondary Christianity not less spiritual, not less heavenly, not less divine than the primary, pretending to a separate and even hostile origin." [1] The author of these excited words, Thomas De Quincey, knew nothing of the Essenes beyond what the ancient Jewish historian Josephus wrote of them, but that little was enough to move him, a century before the Dead Sea Scrolls were discovered, to frame a theory that the Essenes and the earliest Christians were one and the same. De Quincey might well derive a certain satisfaction from the situation today, now that the scrolls of the Essenes, contrary to all reasonable expectations, have come to light. True, his theory seems as fantastic now as it must have then, even though many points of contact between Essene writings and the New Testament have been established; yet he might fairly claim to have had some share of prophetic foreknowledge, if only of the enormous fuss the Essene writings would cause. As one eminent student of the New Testament and the Scrolls has put it: "It is as a potential threat to Christianity, its claims, and its doctrines that the Scrolls have caught the imagination of laymen and clergy." [2] Thus the image of

1. Thomas De Quincey, "The Essenes," *Historical and Critical Essays* (Boston, 1853), p. 116.
2. Krister Stendahl, "The Scrolls and the New Testament: An Introduction and a Perspective," *The Scrolls and the New Testament* (New York, 1957), p. 1.

the double sun, exaggerated though it is, may serve us as an expressive way of symbolizing the importance of these ancient manuscripts and the community that produced them. We now have, if not two suns, at any rate two "new testaments," two religious groups roughly contemporary, each claiming to be the community of the new covenant predicted by Jeremiah. It is irresistible, then, in a study of the covenant, to undertake a comparison of the two and to compare both to earlier manifestations of the idea. Even though this is the history of a *biblical* idea, and the writings of the Essenes are, of course, not scripture, it is unlikely that this, or any future discussion of New Testament ideas, can proceed without consideration of the Dead Sea Scrolls.

Out of the welter of theories and speculations which beclouded early discussion of the Dead Sea Scrolls, a consensus on major points has emerged which is unlikely to be seriously modified, even though publication of the documents is by no means complete. The first finds were made in 1947, in a cave near the Dead Sea. Since then an incredible number of manuscripts have been recovered from ten other caves nearby and from other sites in the general vicinity. Most scholars no longer seriously doubt that these texts formed the library of that party within ancient Judaism called the Essenes, contemporaries of the Pharisees and Sadducees, so that where we once had only the rather meager description of the sect by Josephus and a few other brief ancient notices, now we have their copies of biblical books—itself a sensational advance in our knowledge—and also their own sectarian writings. Excavation has shown that the main center of the group was a complex of buildings near the caves, whose ruins today have the name Khirbet Qumran (hence "Qumran Texts"). The Qumran community seems to have been founded toward the end of the second century B.C. The Essenes lived on in these austere surroundings, and in their other settlements, for a little over a century and a half; but they were involved in the rebellion against Rome and as a group did not survive the campaign in which the tenth Roman legion crushed the uprising. Their center at Qumran was leveled (68 A.D.), and they abandoned their books in the caves near by.

They called themselves "Those who entered the new covenant in the land of Damascus," and although their writings are fascinating from many points of view, we shall have to confine ourselves here to inquiring into the meaning they attached to this phrase, "new covenant." There is almost too much material even on this restricted subject. For a rough measure of the importance of the covenant idea in the sectarian writings from Qumran, we may note that they use the word "covenant" (berit) over five times as often as do the New Testament writers. This abundance of material has suggested the procedure followed here, which is simply to quote at length from the Essene writings. The reader who has followed the history of covenant this far should have little trouble in interpreting the texts for himself, with a minimum of commentary.

The following is from the long scroll often called the Manual of Discipline, which is a kind of constitution for the community. (The main text is from cave I; in a few places, however, the readings of one of the copies from cave IV has been adopted.)[3] (Note that no attempt will be made to trace the further history of the covenant with David. By the time of the Dead Sea Scrolls and the New Testament, this idea survives as part of a complex of Messianic hopes which cannot be treated adequately here.)

3. Variant readings in copies otherwise unpublished are listed in J. T. Milik, review of P. Wernberg-Møller's *The Manual of Discipline, Revue Biblique,* 67 (1960): 412–16.

And when they enter the covenant, the priests and the Levites shall bless the God of salvation, and all his faithful deeds. And when they finish all who are entering the covenant shall say, "Amen, amen!"

Then the priests shall relate the righteous acts of God and his mighty deeds, and proclaim all his unfailing mercies toward Israel. But the Levites are to relate the iniquities of the Israelites, and all the rebellions of which they were guilty, and their sin under the dominion of Belial. When they finish, [all] who are entering the covenant shall confess: "We have done wrong, [we have rebelled, we have sin]ned, we have acted wickedly, we and our fathers before us, in that we went [away from him.] True and righteou[s is] his judgment upon us and on our fathers. But he has granted us his unfailing mercy from everlasting to everlasting.

Then the priests shall bless all the men of the lot of God, those who walk perfect in all his ways, and say, "May he bless you with all good, and keep you from all evil. May he enlighten your mind with understanding unto life, and bestow on you everlasting knowledge. May he lift up his merciful countenance upon you, unto everlasting peace."

Then the Levites shall curse all the men of Belial's lot, and speak up and say, "Be cursed in all your guilty, wicked deeds. May God make you a horror through all the avengers. May he set destruction after you through all who render retribution. Be cursed unmercifully for the darkness of your works and be execrated in the darkness of everlasting fire. May God have no mercy when you cry out, and not forgive and make atonement for your iniquity. May he lift his angry countenance to take vengeance on you, and may no one wish you peace, of all who hold to the fathers." When they are done blessing and cursing, all who enter the covenant shall say, "Amen, amen!"

Then the priests and the Levites shall continue. "Cursed, for the foul idols of his heart . . . be he who enters this covenant but sets the stumbling-block of his iniquity before him so as to go astray, who, when he hears the words of this covenant, blesses himself in his heart and says, 'It will be well with me, though I go on in the stubbornness of my heart,' and his spirit destroy the thirsty with the well-watered, so that he cannot be forgiven. May the wrath of God and his unswerving commands burn against him, unto everlasting destruction. May all the curses of this covenant cleave to him. May God single him out for evil, and may he be cut from the midst of all the Sons of Light for his turning back from after God. For his foul idols and the stumbling block of his iniquity, may he make his lot be in the midst of those cursed forever." Then all who enter the covenant shall say after them, "Amen, amen!"

This shall be performed every year, as long as the dominion of Belial endures (IQS i 18–ii 19).

Now this is the order for the men of the community, for those who have freely chosen to turn from all evil and to hold fast to all which he has commanded as pleasing to him, to be separate from the assembly of perverse men, to be one in sharing the Law, and property; for those who are subject to the will of the sons of Zadok, the priests, the observers of the covenant, and to the will of the multitude of the men of the community, who hold to the covenant. For they shall have authority over every decision on matters of the Law and of property, and of judgment in disputes.

(Their purpose must be) to practice faithfulness in common, and humility; righteousness, and justice, and love of mercy, and humble walking with God in all their ways. No man is to walk in stubbornness of heart, to go astray after his heart, and his eyes, and his evil inclination. Instead, having circumcised in common the foreskin of their will and their stiff neck, to lay a true foundation for Israel, for the community an everlasting covenant. They are to make atonement for all out of Aaron who have freely offered themselves for holiness and for a true house in Israel, and for those joined unto them for common life, and for pleading and judgment of cases, to condemn all who transgress a precept.

The following is the disposition of their conduct with respect to all these precepts having to do with their joining together in a community. Anyone who enters the council of the community does so by entering a covenant with God in the presence of all who have freely offered themselves. He shall swear, by a binding oath, that as he lives he will return to the Law of Moses according to all he commanded, with all his heart and soul. (He shall pledge himself) to all that was revealed out of it to the sons of Zadok, the priests, the observers of the covenant and seekers after his will, and to the multitude of the men in covenant with them, who have freely offered themselves in common to his truth, to walk according to his will. He shall undertake by covenant, that as he lives he will separate from all perverse men, who walk in the way of evil. For they are not counted as being in covenant with him, for they have neither sought nor searched for him in his precepts. Thus they did not find out the hidden things in which they have erred and become guilty; and they have deliberately done wrong in things openly revealed. So wrath has arisen bringing judgment and wreaking of vengeance through the curses of the covenant . . . . For all who have not known his covenant are vanity, and he will blot out of the world all who blaspheme against his word. All their deeds are defiled in his sight, and impurity is in all their property.

When anyone enters into the covenant to do according to all these precepts, and to be united to the holy assembly, they shall jointly and in common investigate his spirit, with respect to his intelligence and his obedience to the Law. This shall be under the authority of the sons of Aaron, those who have freely offered themselves in community to establish his covenant and to see to all the precepts which he commanded men to observe. And (it shall be) under the authority of the multitude of Israel, those who have freely offered to return, in community, to his covenant. The order of them shall be written down, one man following another according to his intelligence and his deeds. This is so that each will be subject to his superior, the lower to the higher, and they shall review their spiritual state and their deeds year by year, so that a man is advanced in keeping with his understanding and the integrity of his conduct, or demoted for his misconduct.

One man is to rebuke another in t[ruth] and humility and kindly love. None is to speak to any of his fellows in anger, or in grumbling, or haughtily, or with an evil, jealous spirit . . . . No man should bring a charge against another before the multitude unless he has (first) asserted it before witnesses. By these they shall walk as long as they are sojourners, every one who remains, each man with his neighbor (IQS v 1–vi 2).

The next passage to be quoted is from the so-called Damascus Document, which is not one of the Dead Sea Scrolls in the strict sense, for the most extensive copies were preserved in a storeroom attached to an ancient synagogue in Cairo and have been known to the scholarly world since 1910. It was, however, only after the more recent finds at Qumran that the work could be satisfactorily understood, and since fragmentary copies have been found at Qumran, it is certain that the work formed part of the Essene library. The first passage quoted is part of an exhortation which states the obligations imposed by the new Essene covenant; the second provides information on how new members were admitted to the covenant.

> (Take care) to do according to the strict sense of the Law during the era of wickedness; and to be separate from the sons of the pit . . . and to distinguish between the unclean and the clean and to teach the distinction between the holy and the profane; and to observe the Sabbath day, according to a strict interpretation, and the set festivals and the day of fasting according to the finding of those who entered the new covenant in the land of Damascus; to set aside the holy offerings, according to strict rules which apply to them; that each man love his brother as himself; to lend a hand to the poor and needy and the alien; that each should seek the welfare of his brother; and that none should betray his own flesh and blood;
> to keep away from prostitutes according to the rule;
> that a man should reprove his brother according to the commandment and not bear a grudge from one day to the next;
> and to be separate from all unclean things according to the rules pertaining to them, so that no man should defile his holy spirit, just as God set them apart.
> All who walk in these (precepts), in holy integrity subject to all the admonitions of the [covenant], the covenant of God shall be confirmed for them to give them life (for) a thousand generations (CD vi 14–vii 6).[4]

> The sons of any member of the covenant (granted) to all Israel as an everlasting ordinance, when they reach the age for being enrolled formally, shall be made to take an oath of the covenant.
> And so also shall be the practice, during the whole era of wickedness with anyone who turns from his corrupt way,

4. The Hebrew text is especially difficult here, and there are divergences in the copies; I have followed for the most part the "A" text as emended by Chaim Rabin, *The Zadokite Documents*, 2d ed. (Oxford, 1958), p. 27.

at the time when he speaks with the overseer of the multitude, that is, he shall be enrolled by an oath of the covenant
which Moses made with Israel, a covenant to [return t]o the
Law of Moses with all his heart and soul (CD xv 5–10).

In all this, and in the rest of Essene literature as well,
there is a great deal that is thoroughly familiar to a student
of Old Testament language about covenant. Not only are
the terms the same as Old Testament terms, which might
have been expected, but they are also used to convey covenant concepts of very great antiquity. There is, first of all,
the basic idea that the covenant involves an oath, which is
fundamental to most Old Testament uses of the term. The
texts quoted above are sufficient to show that the Essene
covenant rested on an oath by each member of the community, administered and renewed in the most formal way
possible, but it may be interesting to see how this is restated
in one of the *Hodayot*, or Thanksgiving Hymns, a poem
composed, in all likelihood, by the founder of the community:

By a solemn oath I have undertaken not to sin against thee
    And not to do anything evil in thy sight.
So also I have brought all men of my council
    into a community.
                (IQH xiv 17–18)

There is a reminiscence of the historical introduction
to the covenant in the order for entering the covenant
quoted above: at the beginning the priests recite "the righteous acts of God and his mighty deeds," and the Levites
respond by relating "the iniquities of the Israelites . . .
under the dominion of Belial" (a name for Satan). Even
in such a brief compass as this passage, new and peculiarly
sectarian emphases make their appearance: the tendency to
see everything in a dualistic way, that is, as exemplifying a
clash and contrast between good and evil, and the stress on
predestination and the division of history into eras with a

predetermined character ("the dominion of Belial"). Thus it is doubtful that the Essenes understood or used the history of God's saving acts in exactly the same way as the early Israelites. Even so, there is a surprising fidelity to the ancient form.

Much the same may be said of another feature of the ancient form which was maintained among the Qumran sectarians, the blessings and curses. Though it was used, it was changed, for the old idea was that blessing and curse applied to the same man or community; they were the life or death alternatives which the members of the covenant confronted. This is blurred at Qumran; the blessings are for those within the covenant, and the curses are for those on the outside, "the men of Belial's lot." Their extreme form of predestinarian belief divided mankind into those elected to covenant and those chosen for perdition under the dominion of Satan, and this shifted their understanding of blessing and curse. True enough, they did hold out dire threats for anyone who would betray his oath and fall back to darkness. "All those men who entered the new covenant in the land of Damascus, and have turned around and been unfaithful and have left the spring of living waters, shall not be reckoned in the council of the people, or included when they are written down" (CD viii 21). Even though this concept is present, however, it is overshadowed by the radical division of mankind into the sons of light and the sons of darkness, and the resemblance to the old idea, although close, is mostly formal.

Two other familiar covenant themes make their appearance. One is that the covenant involves obligations on the part of those within it, and the other is that the covenant must be renewed periodically. In the case of the Essenes, this was a yearly rite held on the Feast of Weeks, that is, Pentecost.

Thus, as Mendenhall has pointed out,[5] the Essene covenant is much like the covenant that accompanied the reform
of Josiah, or the covenant under Ezra. It is the charter of
a repristination movement. At the heart is the familiar idea
of return: "(A man) shall swear, by a binding oath that as
he lives he will return to the Law of Moses according to all
he commanded, with all his heart and soul." Covenant is
understood as an oath of loyalty to an established set of
precepts, as interpreted by a clearly defined authority, the
Zadokite priests. This is not to say that there was nothing
new or creative in Essene thought; for they innovated in
many ways—indeed it is probably true that anyone who
wants to re-create old ways is compelled to innovate. Nor,
in stressing the legalistic character of the Essene covenant,
do I mean to suggest that the covenant was unable to evoke
sincere religious feeling in those who stood within it. On
the contrary, the Thanksgiving Hymns amply attest the depth
and fervor of the emotion which the pact with God aroused
in their author. "I thank Thee, O Lord, because thou hast
enlightened my face by thy covenant" (IQH iv 5), he writes
at the head of one of his psalms; elsewhere he compares
the covenant to the water of life (v 9). It is safe to assume
that his feelings of awe and joy and gratitude at being in
league with God were shared by the rest of the community.
Yet for all their sincerity, Essene ideas about covenant are
essentially conservative and recapitulate familiar patterns.
Their new covenant is a renewal of the old.

"In many and various ways God spoke of old to our
fathers by the prophets; but in these last days he has spoken
to us by a Son, whom he appointed the heir of all things,

5. For the discussion of covenant at Qumran and in the New
Testament the present writer is heavily indebted to the treatment by
George Mendenhall, "Covenant," *The Interpreter's Dictionary of the
Bible* (New York and Nashville, 1962), 1: 721–23.

through whom also he created the world" (Hebrews 1:1–2).[6] This first sentence of the letter to the Hebrews (of unknown authorship, but not by Paul) says nothing about covenant, yet it says a great deal about the conceptual framework within which New Testament use of the term must be understood. Note first the sharp separation of sacred history into two periods. Early Christians, even those of Jewish descent, did not look on themselves either as an unbroken continuation of the old Israel or as a group attempting to return to an ancient pattern of faith, like the Essenes. Instead, they stood over against the days "of old" as men living in the "last days." This setting of new against old has its counterpart in the mode of God's revelation: of old it came through the prophetic word; now it has come through a person, a Son. Most significant for our purpose is the contrasting of the plurality of modes of revelation under the old dispensation to the single channel under the new. As elaborated by the writer to the Hebrews, this means that feature after feature of Old Testament religion must be seen as prefiguring a single person, Jesus Christ. To use the terminology theologians later applied, he comes as the single antitype in whom is fulfilled the significance of a host of types. Thus if God has appointed him "the heir of all things," it is no surprise to find that he is the heir of the covenant idea also; that is, that the new covenant is understood as involving a person, Jesus Christ, in a way quite unlike anything we have seen so far.

To show that Jesus brings a "better" covenant, one "enacted on better promises," Hebrews quotes in full Jeremiah's prophecy of the new covenant and then asserts flatly,

6. Quotations from the New Testament are from the Revised Standard Version of the Bible, copyright 1946 and 1952 by the Division of Christian Education, National Council of the Churches of Christ in the U.S.A., and are reprinted by permission.

"In speaking of a new covenant, he treats the first as obsolete. And what is becoming obsolete and growing old is ready to vanish away" (8:13). Elaboration of the idea and justification for this adjective "better" is supplied in a later passage, 9:11–23:

> But when Christ appeared as a high priest of the good things that have come, then through the greater and more perfect tent (not made with hands, that is, not of this creation) he entered once for all into the Holy Place, taking not the blood of goats and calves but his own blood, thus securing an eternal redemption. For if the sprinkling of defiled persons with the blood of goats and bulls and with the ashes of a heifer sanctifies for the purification of the flesh, how much more shall the blood of Christ, who through the eternal Spirit offered himself without blemish to God, purify your conscience from dead works to serve the living God. Therefore he is the mediator of a new covenant [diatheke], so that those who are called may receive the promised eternal inheritance, since a death has occurred which redeems them from the transgressions under the first covenant [diatheke]. For where a will [diatheke] is involved, the death of the one who made it must be established. For a will [diatheke] takes effect only at death, since it is not in force as long as the one who made it is alive. Hence even the first covenant [diatheke] was not ratified without blood. For when every commandment of the law had been declared by Moses to all the people, he took the blood of calves and goats, with water and scarlet wool and hyssop, and sprinkled both the book itself and all the people, saying, "This is the blood of the covenant [diatheke] which God commanded you." And in the same way he sprinkled with the blood both the tent and all the vessels used in worship. Indeed, under the law almost everything is purified with blood, and without the shedding of blood there is no forgiveness of sins. Thus it was necessary for the copies of the heavenly things to be purified with these rites, but the heavenly things themselves with better sacrifices than these.

High priest, tent, blood, sacrifice, covenant: every term here is old, yet each is transmuted. Each has become a way of asserting what happened through Christ. A helpful way to grasp the nature of the change that has taken place is to think of the phrase "mediator of the new covenant."

A rather obvious comparison is implied: Jesus is another Moses, who was the mediator, or go-between, for the old covenant. But the incongruity of the comparison is as striking as its appropriateness. However prominent Moses is in traditions about Sinai, he is always the messenger of Yahweh. Though Moses' face shone after he came down from the mountain, it was with reflected glory, and it was possible for Israel to recite the people's sacred history without mentioning Moses. In the New Testament, things are the other way around, and this text from Hebrews shows that covenant has become one way among many of describing what happened through Jesus Christ.

The writer's play with the biblical Greek word for covenant, *diatheke*, is significant in this connection. The word *diatheke* in ordinary Greek means "disposition (of property), testament, (last) will." This word was chosen by the translators who prepared the Septuagint, the Greek version of the Old Testament, as an equivalent for Hebrew *berit*, which never means "last will and testament." It is not altogether clear why they did this, though they may have meant to stress that *berit* often does refer to a one-sided disposition of things by God. Whatever the reason, this introduced an ambiguity which the writer to the Hebrews, like Paul (Galatians 3:15) and before him the Jewish philosopher and apologist, Philo of Alexandria, was happy to exploit. To show how Christ's death benefits men, giving them an "eternal inheritance," and to connect this with Old Testament thought, he uses the nonbiblical sense of *diatheke*, "last will and testament," which permits him to introduce the idea that for a will to take effect "the death of the one who made it must be established," and so on. It would be beside the point to object that this is bad philology, that the mere verbal shell of an ancient concept is retained and filled with alien contents, for the writer to the Hebrews was not below the standards of his time in these matters.

The point worth noting is that the death of Jesus has suggested the meaning he attaches to *diatheke,* "covenant," and not the reverse.

To employ still another approach to this passage in Hebrews we may ask, How much is left here of the ancient concept of the covenant as an oath sworn by a man which places him under strict obligation and under a curse if he is faithless? The answer is obvious. At least at this point in the book these essential features of the old covenant are absent. Christ so dominates the conception that there is little attention paid to the role of the human partners in the covenant. Later, however, something rather like the old idea of the curse comes to the fore. "A man who has violated the law of Moses dies without mercy at the testimony of two or three witnesses. How much worse punishment do you think will be deserved by the man who has spurned the Son of God, and profaned the blood of the covenant by which he was sanctified, and outraged the Spirit of grace?" (10:28–29). The blood of Jesus, otherwise thought of as the means for bringing forgiveness of sins, is introduced here in a different context; it involves the sinner in guilt to a degree immeasurably greater than the guilt brought on by transgression of the old law. It is probably correct to see in this passage a distant echo of the old conception in which the covenant partner brought a conditional curse on himself through the "blood of the covenant." Yet this conception is relatively rare, and curses were a much more prominent part of the Essene covenant than of the Christian conception.

In using the idea of a new covenant to explain what happened in Christ, Paul follows the same path as the writer to the Hebrews, yet his emphasis is different. In Hebrews the stress is on the new as foreshadowed in the old. The new covenant is better than the Sinai covenant, but it does not contradict it; it fulfills it and reveals its deepest meaning. In Paul, on the other hand, the two are contrasted so sharply that there is no apparent continuity left between the Sinai covenant and the new covenant in Christ, and the apostle has to reach back to the covenant with Abraham as an anticipation for his gospel and has to elaborate the view that the Sinai covenant is only an episode, an interruption in the history of faith. This polarizing tendency in Paul's use of "covenant" appears in very characteristic form in II Corinthians 3. Although a table can give only the skeleton of his thought, it has the advantage of showing in a simple way how for Paul the new covenant is the opposite of the old.

Old Covenant (Sinai)	New Covenant
written on tables of stone	written on human hearts
a written code	Spirit of the living God
kills	gives life
a dispensation of death	dispensation of the Spirit
condemnation	righteousness
fading	permanent
veiled glory	direct view of God's glory

Another highly characteristic passage in which Paul uses "covenant" is Galatians 3, which is especially interesting because Paul takes up here the question involved in his radical distinction between the promise to Abraham and the "law" given at Sinai: Is the law then against the promises of God? But to follow Paul's thought through this chapter, or through the odd and involved allegory of the next, which speaks of two covenants under the figures of Sarah and Hagar, Isaac and Ishmael, the present Jerusalem and the Jerusalem above, would lead too far from the central concern of this book. Paul is not really talking about covenant but is presenting a new drama of ideas: faith and works, law and gospel, are the main actors, and covenant comes in only to swell a scene or two. It is relatively easy to remark that in identifying the Sinai covenant as "law," Paul scarcely does justice to its full content; but it is equally obvious that such an academic point is not really the issue.

Paul and the writer to the Hebrews were theologians and used the idea of covenant at the level of theological debate and exposition. Even though their writings were probably more intelligible to their contemporaries than are those of most modern theologians, they do not give us much insight into what "covenant" meant to ordinary early Christians in their thinking of themselves and their church. Did the followers of Jesus, like the Israelites of old, or the Essenes of their own day, commonly think of themselves as joined to God and to one another by a solemn oath? Our best New Testament evidence on this subject is the church's traditions about the Last Supper, the words Jesus spoke and the actions he performed as he ate with his disciples in anticipation of his death and spoke of a new covenant in his blood. Here "covenant" stands in a context obviously close to the heart of the Christian faith, in a tradition that from very early times must have been universally used in Christian instruction and worship. Within the narrow compass of the New Testament there are four passages that contain the eucharistic words of Jesus, one each in the gospels according to Matthew (26:26–29), Mark (14:22–25), and Luke (22:15–20), and one in Paul's first letter to the Corinthians (11:23–25). Even though this last stands within a letter by Paul, two things certify that even here we are not dealing with some special Pauline interpretation of the eucharist but with ancient and general tradition—first, the solemn introduction: "For I received from the Lord what I also delivered to you"; and second, the context: Paul was trying to deal with particularly gross offenses in regard to the sacrament, in a church that had its doubts about his authority as an apostle. Thus we may be sure he is at this point speaking as impersonally as possible.

Yet even though we are in the very unusual situation of having four versions from which to study this new covenant, there are serious difficulties involved in reconstructing and interpreting what was said and done by Jesus and how it was understood by his disciples. The first difficulty is that we cannot be completely certain about what kind of meal this was and thus cannot with complete confidence interpret Jesus' words against the background of the Passover celebration or any other solemn meal known to us. The synoptic gospels, that is, the first three, which closely resemble one another at a great many points, seem to make the Last Supper a Passover meal, but the gospel of John puts it on the day before the Passover. The question as to which is correct and the related problems make up one of the most complicated and controversial areas in all biblical studies. It would be pointless to go into more detail here, for even another monograph is not apt to settle the problem; even fresh evidence from Qumran has not yielded a universally convincing harmonization. Nor do the four versions of the eucharistic words agree so closely that it is possible to be sure about the original form, or about which of them is closest to it. The account given by St. Luke is the most widely divergent, since according to Luke, Jesus first takes a cup, blesses and distributes it, then bread, and then, according to most ancient manuscripts, another cup, which is "the new covenant in my blood," whereas one famous and rather eccentric early manuscript, Codex Bezae (D), and the old Latin translation leave out the second cup-saying altogether. Instead of setting ourselves the ambitious goal of reconstructing the original sequence of events and restoring the very syllables spoken by Jesus, we are better advised to go a different way and to study all four, in their variety, as witnesses to different ways in which early Christians portrayed the meaning of the new covenant.[7] Since we have adopted this inclusive method, we will go even farther and take in some of what John's gospel says about the Last Supper, even though his account says nothing explicit about the eucharist or a new covenant.

The most obvious tie to older covenant traditions is in the words "new covenant" (Luke 22:20; I Corinthians 11:25), which refers to the prophecy of Jeremiah (31:31–34) of a new covenant "not like the covenant which I made with their fathers." Matthew (26:28) underlines this tie and comments on it: the blood is "poured out for many for the forgiveness of sins," which echoes Jeremiah's "For I will forgive their iniquity, and I will remember their sin no more."

Since Jeremiah's prophecy is the one Old Testament passage about covenant drawn on most directly here, it is likely that the eucharistic words are using "covenant" in much the same way that Jeremiah did at this one point, that is, to refer to a binding order of things established by God and based on the forgiveness of sins. It would be pushing beyond the evidence to read into Jesus' words much more of the ancient conceptions associated with covenant.

This is true in spite of the fact that the eucharistic words also refer to the blood of the covenant, which is a quotation from Exodus 24:8, in the pericope dealing with the Sinai covenant. In Luke and Paul the form of words is: "This cup is the new covenant in my blood," whereas Mark

7. In a famous letter of Pliny the Younger to the Emperor Trajan (Book X, no. 96 of Pliny's letters, from about A.D. 111), Pliny passes on to the emperor information about the practices of the Christians which he had extracted from lapsed members of the sect. In spite of its great interest, I omit discussion of the letter. The key passage, which says that Christians bound themselves by an oath (Latin sacramentum) not to commit evil acts, presents many difficulties. For a discussion and review of the extensive literature about the letter, see A. N. Sherwin-White, *The Letters of Pliny: A Historical and Social Commentary* (Oxford, 1966), pp. 691–710.

and Matthew have a curious phrasing: "This is my blood of the new covenant," which is often thought to be a later form, influenced by its counterpart, "This is my body." This reference to blood is covenant language of very ancient line-age, but the idea is at least half-new. In Moses' use of the words "blood of the covenant," the blood helps bring the curse into effect; the people are identified with the victim, whose fate will be theirs if they sin. The eucharistic words do indeed identify Jesus with his disciples—note that all the versions, at one point or another, have "for you," "on your behalf," or the like—but the emphasis is not on bringing them under a curse but rather of a sacrifice made on their behalf. Thus, though there is a verbal echo of the Sinai covenant, the real conceptual link is to the new covenant of forgiveness of which Jeremiah spoke.

Other resemblances to the form or intent of any of the old covenants are hard to find. Mendenhall would find a counterpart to the covenant history, the recital of the gracious acts of God, in the fact that Jesus made the covenant in an-ticipation of his death and that the Christian community re-membered that saving event in later ritual repetitions of the Lord's Supper. One may also bring in, as Mendenhall does, the "new commandment" given by Jesus according to John's Last Supper account: "A new commandment I give to you, that you love one another; even as I have loved you, that you also love one another" (John 13:34). This may be taken as showing an association of "new covenant" with "new com-mandment," just as the old covenant had its stipulations, the commandments. And there is an even more direct reminis-cence in Paul of another ancient covenant element, the curse: "Whoever, therefore, eats the bread or drinks the cup of the Lord in an unworthy manner will be guilty of pro-faning the body and blood of the Lord" (I Corinthians 11:27). This follows his quotation of the eucharistic words.

Yet note in each of these how the person of Jesus has, so to speak, taken over the original notion: the saving event is *his* death, the new commandment is to love in imitation of *his* example, the guilt of abusing communion is that one has profaned *his* body and blood. One need only compare the Essene "new covenant" to see that these two are very different growths, even if they come from the same soil. The Essenes had a covenant, but it was not new; the Christians had something new, but it was not a covenant. That is to say, to call what Jesus brought a covenant is like calling conversion circumcision, or like saying that one keeps the Passover with the unleavened bread of sincerity and truth. For Christians, the coming of the substance made shadows out of a rich array of Old Testament events, persons, and ideas, among them covenant. *Figuram res exterminat;*[8] the reality brings the image to an end.

8. The phrase is from a stanza by Adam of St. Victor: *Jam scisso velo patuit / Quod vetus lex praecinuit; / Figuram res exterminat / Et umbram lux illuminat. The Liturgical Poetry of Adam of St. Victor*, ed. Wrangham (London, 1881), I: 60; quoted in Don Cameron Allen, *Image and Meaning*, new enl. ed. (Baltimore, 1968), p. 142.

SUGGESTIONS FOR FURTHER READING

General Works on the Old Testament and the History of Israel

ALBRIGHT, W. F. *The Biblical Period from Abraham to Ezra.* New York: Harper & Row, 1963. Harper Torchbooks TB 102.

ANDERSON, BERNHARD W. *Understanding the Old Testament.* Englewood Cliffs, N. J.: Prentice-Hall, 1957.

BRIGHT, JOHN. *A History of Israel.* Philadelphia: Westminster, 1959.

DRIVER, S. R. *An Introduction to the Literature of the Old Testament.* New York: Meridian Books, 1956. This classic work first appeared in 1898.

GOTTWALD, N. K. *A Light to the Nations: An Introduction to the Old Testament.* New York: Harper & Brothers, 1959.

HAHN, H. F. *The Old Testament in Modern Research,* with a survey of recent literature by Horace Hummel. Philadephia: Fortress Press, 1966.

NOTH, MARTIN. *The History of Israel.* 2d rev. ed. New York: Harper & Brothers, 1960.

DE VAUX, ROLAND. *Ancient Israel: Its Life and Institutions.* New York: McGraw-Hill, 1961. Two-volume paperback edition in McGraw-Hill paperbacks nos. 16599 and 16600.

WEISER, A. *The Old Testament: Its Formation and Development.* New York: Association Press, 1961.

WELLHAUSEN, JULIUS. *Prolegomena to the History of Ancient Israel.* New York: World, 1957. Meridian Paperback MG 35.
A translation of Wellhausen's influential work on the history of Israelite religion.

WRIGHT, G. E., and FULLER, R. H. *The Book of the Acts of God*. Garden City, N. Y.: Doubleday, 1960. Anchor Books A 222.

On the History of Biblical Interpretation

FARRAR, F. W. *History of Interpretation*. London: Macmillan, 1886. Recently reprinted by Baker Book House, Grand Rapids, Mich.

GRANT, ROBERT M. *A Short History of the Interpretation of the Bible*. Rev. ed. New York: Macmillan, 1963.

GREENSLADE, S. L., ed. *The Cambridge History of the Bible: The West from the Reformation to the Present Day*. Cambridge: Cambridge University Press, 1963.

SMALLEY, B. *The Study of the Bible in the Middle Ages*. 2d ed. London: Basil Blackwell, 1952. Paperback edition by University of Notre Dame Press, 1964, NDP 39.

STRACK, HERMANN L. *Introduction to the Talmud and Midrash*. New York: Meridian Books and the Jewish Publication Society of America, 1959.
A translation of an older work dealing with early Jewish interpretation.

On Biblical Archaeology and the Old Testament World

ALBRIGHT, W. F. *From the Stone Age to Christianity*. 2d ed. Baltimore: Johns Hopkins Press, 1957. Also available in Doubleday Anchor Books A 100.

――――. *Archaeology and the Religion of Israel*. Baltimore: Johns Hopkins Press, 1942.
Especially valuable for its account of Canaanite religion.

Biblical Archaeologist, published quarterly by the American Schools of Oriental Research, Jerusalem and Baghdad, is a periodical containing first-hand popular accounts by archaeologists of the latest archaeological researches bearing on the Bible.

GRAY, JOHN. *The Canaanites*. London: Thames and Hudson, 1964. Ancient Peoples and Places, no. 38.

GURNEY, O. R. *The Hittites.* Harmondsworth: Penguin, 1954. Penguin A 259.

KRAMER, S. N. *The Sumerians: Their History, Culture, and Character.* Chicago: University of Chicago Press, 1963.

NOTH, MARTIN. *The Old Testament World.* Philadelphia: Fortress Press, 1966.

OPPENHEIM, A. L. *Ancient Mesopotamia: Portrait of a Dead Civilization.* Chicago: University of Chicago Press, 1964.

WILSON, J. A. *The Culture of Ancient Egypt.* Chicago: University of Chicago Press, 1951. Phoenix Books P 11.

WRIGHT, G. E. *Biblical Archaeology.* 2d ed. Philadelphia: Westminster, 1961; and London: G. Duckworth, 1962.

On Treaties and Covenants

HILLERS, DELBERT R. *Treaty-Curses and the Old Testament Prophets.* Biblica et Orientalia, no. 16. Rome: Pontifical Biblical Institute, 1964.

McCARTHY, D. J., S.J. *Treaty and Covenant: A Study in the Ancient Oriental Documents and in the Old Testament.* Analecta Biblica, no. 21. Rome: Pontifical Biblical Institute, 1963.
Contains translations of some treaties.

MENDENHALL, GEORGE E. *Law and Covenant in Israel and the Ancient Near East.* Pittsburgh: The Biblical Colloquium, 1955.

———. "Covenant," *The Interpreter's Dictionary of the Bible.* Vol. I, edited by G. A. Buttrick. New York and Nashville: Abingdon, 1962.

PRITCHARD, J. B., ed. *Ancient Near Eastern Texts Relating to the Old Testament.* 2d ed. Princeton: Princeton University Press, 1954.
This work includes translations of some important treaties.

On the Dead Sea Scrolls and the Qumran Community

CROSS, FRANK MOORE, JR. *The Ancient Library of Qumran and Modern Biblical Studies.* Rev. ed. Garden City, N.Y.: Doubleday, 1961. Anchor Books A 272.

MILIK, J. T. *Ten Years of Discovery in the Wilderness of Judaea.* Studies in Biblical Theology, no. 26. London: SCM Press, 1959.

VERMES, G. *The Dead Sea Scrolls in English.* Harmondsworth: Penguin, 1962. Pelican A 551.

Additional Suggestions for Further Reading, 1977

Important new translations of some Hittite and Akkadian treaties, prepared by the late Albrecht Goetze and by Erica Reiner, appear in James B. Pritchard, ed., *Ancient Near Eastern Texts.* Third edition, revised, with supplement. Princeton: Princeton University Press, 1969. Pp. 529–41.

The following works will enable the reader to survey later developments in study of the covenant idea in Israel, and to consider differing points of view.

CROSS, FRANK MOORE. "A Brief Excursus on bĕrīt, 'Covenant,' " in his *Canaanite Myth and Hebrew Epic: Essays in the History of the Religion of Israel.* Cambridge, Mass.: Harvard University Press, 1973. Pp. 265–73.

McCARTHY, D. J. *Old Testament Covenant: A Survey of Current Opinions.* Richmond: John Knox, 1973.

RIEMANN, P. A. "Covenant, Mosaic," in *The Interpreter's Dictionary of the Bible, Supplementary Volume,* ed. Keith Crim. Nashville: Abingdon, 1976. Pp. 192–97.

WEINFELD, MOSHE. "The Covenant of Grant in the Old Testament and in the Ancient Near East," *Journal of the American Oriental Society* 90 (1970): 184–203.

———. "Covenant." *Encyclopaedia Judaica.* New York: Macmillan, 1971. V, cols. 1011–22.

———. "Covenant, Davidic." *The Interpreter's Dictionary of the Bible, Supplementary Volume,* ed. Keith Crim. Nashville: Abingdon, 1976. Pp. 188–92.

INDEX OF SCRIPTURE REFERENCES

Designed by Edward King

Composed in Linotype Electra by The Colonial Press Inc.

Printed offset on P&S Old Forge by The Colonial Press Inc.

Bound in paper and cloth editions by The Colonial Press Inc.